Dorothy

To remind y
Visit to Oxford ....   —
28th February 2012

The
INKLINGS
of
OXFORD

Also by Harry Lee Poe

C. S. Lewis Remembered (with Rebecca Whitten Poe)

What God Knows (with J. Stanley Mattson)

See No Evil: The Existence of Evil in an Age of Relativism

Christianity in the Academy: Teaching at the Intersection of Faith and Learning

Designer Universe: Intelligent Design and the Existence of God

Christian Witness in a Postmodern World

Science and Faith: An Evangelical Dialogue (with Jimmy H. Davis)

The Gospel and Its Meaning

The Fruit of Christ's Presence

C.S. Lewis,
J.R.R. Tolkien,
and Their Friends

The INKLINGS of OXFORD

TEXT BY

HARRY LEE POE

PHOTOGRAPHY BY

JAMES RAY VENEMAN

ZONDERVAN®

ZONDERVAN.com/
AUTHORTRACKER
follow your favorite authors

ZONDERVAN®

The Inklings of Oxford
Copyright © 2009 by Harry Lee Poe

Requests for information should be addressed to:
Zondervan, *Grand Rapids, Michigan 49530*

Library of Congress Cataloging-in-Publication Data

Poe, Harry Lee, 1950 –
     The Inklings of Oxford : a pictorial account / text by Harry Lee Poe ; photography by Jim Veneman.
          p. cm.
     Includes bibliographical references and index.
     ISBN 978-0-310-28503-8 (pbk.)
     1. Inklings (Group of writers) 2. Inklings (Group of writers) — Pictorial works. 3. Authors, English — Homes and haunts — England — Oxford. 4. Authors, English — Homes and haunts — England — Oxford — Pictorial works. 5. Oxford (England) — Intellectual life — 20th century. 6. Oxford (England) — Biography. 7. Oxford (England) — Pictorial works. 8. University of Oxford — Biography. 9. University of Oxford — Pictorial works.
     I. Veneman, Jim, 1952 – II. Title.
     PR478.I54P64 2008
     820.9'00912 — dc22

                                                                                                                2008042453

Interior design by Michelle Espinoza

Printed in China

09 10 11 12 13 14 • 23 22 21 20 19 18 17 16 15 14 13 12 11 10 9 8 7 6 5 4 3 2 1

CONTENTS

PREFACE

When I first went up to Oxford in 1979 to "read" the English Puritans with Barrie White, I had never read the Chronicles of Narnia or the Lord of the Rings. I had never heard of the Inklings. I had heard of Tolkien and his Hobbits (who didn't wear shoes and had hairy feet) during my undergraduate days in the late 1960s. It all sounded subversive to me then. As for Lewis, I did not understand why my friends in seminary, grown men no less, should get so excited about children's stories. The summer before going to Oxford, however, while serving as a prison chaplain, I decided to take a week and read one of the Narnia books each day. They proved charming.

When I went to Oxford, my friends who were so excited about Lewis and Tolkien asked if I would mind showing one of their friends around Oxford when I got settled. A few weeks later, a woman named Anne Coppenger came to town from Scotland, where she had been teaching. I was

Anne Coppenger beside the old city walls of Oxford in the gardens of New College where Lord David Cecil and Christopher Tolkien were fellows

J. R. R. Tolkien (© Copyright Billett Potter, Oxford)

C. S. Lewis (Used by permission of The Marion E. Wade Center, Wheaton College, Wheaton, IL.)

at Regent's Park College in St. Giles, which shares a common wall with the Eagle and Child pub, and Anne stayed in the little hotel that then occupied the building at the corner of Pusey Street and St. Giles, where the Tolkiens first lived in Oxford. As it turned out, I did not show Anne around. Instead, she gave me the tour that eventually turned into this book.

Along the way I have written a number of articles about Lewis and Tolkien. The first reviews I ever wrote for scholarly journals were of Walter Hooper's *Through Joy and Beyond* and the Clyde Kilby and Marjorie Mead edition of Warren Lewis's diary. I have taught a course on Lewis for several years. I have enjoyed the company of the C. S. Lewis Society of Memphis for many years. I have had the pleasure of meeting many of Lewis's former students, which led to the publication of a volume of essays entitled *C. S. Lewis Remembered*, a book I edited with my daughter, Rebecca. I had the pleasure of leading a seminar on Apologetics in a Postmodern Age for the 1998 C. S. Lewis Summer Institute, where I met Chuck Colson, who credits Lewis as playing a major role in his own conversion. Several years later, Colson lent his name and the support of Prison Fellowship to the professorship I now hold. In 2002 and 2005 I was invited by Stan Mattson, president of the C. S. Lewis Foundation, to serve as program director for the C. S. Lewis Summer Institute. I do not consider myself a C. S. Lewis scholar, but I have noted that Lewis appears prominently in the index of twelve of the fifteen books I have written. His insights have informed my scholarship about the gospel and culture. And it all began with Anne Coppenger, to whom and for whom I am most grateful.

Now for the punch line. I had been waiting for years for someone to do this book, and having lost patience, I decided to do it myself. I wanted to see the places I had visited, but more, I wanted those who have grown to love the Inklings through their writings to see the town where they lived and worked and played. Several fine books have been written about the Inklings in addition to the fine biographies of individual members. But I wanted a picture book for the average person. I thought about taking the pictures myself for almost three minutes. Vanity passed and my mind fixed on Jim Veneman, a truly gifted artist with a camera. He immediately agreed to a collaboration, and we spent ten days in August 2007 taking the shots. While sitting beside the river at the Trout one evening, eating a splendid meal, Jim reminded me that he had attended Ouachita University in Arkansas. I remembered that Anne Coppenger's father had taught philosophy at Ouachita, and I asked Jim if he knew of Dr. Coppenger. A huge smile crossed his face, and for the next thirty minutes he told me about the extraordinary Coppenger family and how much they had meant to so many students over so many years. So, to the Coppengers, Jim and I both thank you.

Beyond the Coppengers, we have many others who played a role in the development and completion of this book. David Frees, our editor at Zondervan, took the idea through the approval process and helped us shape the book as a visual experience and not just a collection of words. Bob Hudson, who edited my last Lewis book with Zondervan, edited the text and coordinated the continuity of text, photographs, and maps with Mark Sheeres, Rob Monacelli, and Kim Zeilstra. David Dockery, the president of Union University, which employs both of us, has been encouraging and generous in his support of this project. Several old friends and several new friends took time to meet with us and discuss the project. We are most grateful to Derek Brewer, Barbara Reynolds, Francis Warner, George Watson, Basil Mitchell, Brown Patterson, Paul Fiddes, and Walter Hooper. Colin Duriez, who has written several important books on Lewis, Tolkien, and the Inklings, graciously took us out to Headington to see Hillsboro House, where Lewis lived with Mrs. Moore. We are grateful to Heidi Truty at Wheaton College's Wade Center for her diligent research into the photographs of the Inklings themselves; to Billett Potter for permission to use his classic, incomparable photos of J. R. R. Tolkien; and to Tolkien scholar Pieter Collier for his invaluable research assistance and advice. John Bowen and Don King always offered helpful insights and valuable criticism that are the gift of friendship.

Walter Hooper shows us the photographs he took of Lewis at the Kilns in 1963.

Colin Duriez in the taxi when he took us to Hillsboro House

Stan Mattson at the Kilns

We have been mindful that most of the places associated with the Inklings are private institutions, so we are most grateful for permission to take photographs granted to the public by Merton College, New College, Exeter College, the Bodleian Library, St. Mary the Virgin Church, Holy Trinity Church, Magdalene College, Holywell Music Room, and the Sheldonian Theatre. We are grateful to Mark Blandford-Baker, Home Bursar of Magdalen College, for permission to take photographs within the college. We are grateful to Ruth Dry, Bursar's PA and Fellows' Secretary of Keble College, for facilitating permission to take photographs within Keble. We are grateful to Helen Morton, Treasurer of Somerville College, for permission to take photographs at Somerville College. We are grateful to Stan Mattson for permission to take photographs at the Kilns. The staff of the Eagle and Child cheerfully allowed us to take their pictures while they went about their duties, and we appreciate their kindness.

When I planned this book, I knew that Jim and I could not take all the pictures we needed during a shoot in August. We are most fortunate to have two younger (at our age, everybody is younger) colleagues who have contributed some important photographs to the book to make it complete. Ben Dockery studied in Oxford in 2005 and provided several of his pictures. Rebecca Whitten Poe studied in Oxford in Michaelmas term 2007. We are grateful for their contributions.

Our wives, Mary Anne Poe and Carol Veneman, have seen us distracted during the tight schedule within which we worked to finish this book. They have always been gracious, but we do not take their graciousness for granted. We thank them for their encouragement and support of this project that we hope will bring some joy and encouragement to those who read it and view the town the Inklings loved.

HARRY LEE POE
JACKSON, TENNESSEE
OCTOBER 15, 2007

INTRODUCTION

This book is not an ordinary book. It is both a picture book and a storybook. It tells all about a place and the friends who lived there. What makes the book special, though, is that it is not only about that place and those friends; it is also about you.

Everyone needs a special place all their own, even if they do not own it. Everyone needs friends who are always there, even if they are not there with us. What makes a place special for a person does not depend upon the place, but upon the person. What makes a person special is not so much the person, but the people who think they are special: their friends.

A person's high school or college may forever be the most special place because of the friends who made that place special. At an

Tourists now eat their lunches in the garden of St. Mary the Virgin Church.
(Photo by Ben Dockery)

important time in life when people were changing from children into grownups, a few people shared in the amazing transformation. While the places where we live and work do not define us or determine who and what we will become, they do form the context

Opposite page: Blackwell's Bookshop, arguably the greatest book store in the world, stands on Broad Street between the White Horse and the King's Arms where the Inklings often visited during the beer shortages of World War II.

in which we flourish, wither, or merely subsist. The places of our lives either nourish us or drain us. Places do not make us, but they provide the physical space in which we relate to the people who play such an important role, for good or ill, in shaping who we become. The special place of this book is the university and city of Oxford. The special people are a group of friends who lived there and called themselves the Inklings.

THE CITY OF OXFORD

Oxford has been a remarkable place for a thousand years and has attracted fascinating people for each of those years. Around every corner and along every street, the echoes of its rich history abound. Walk under the Bridge of Sighs opposite the Bodleian Library, look to the left, and there stands the house, with its observation platform on top, where Edmund Halley made his astronomical observations and predicted the return of the comet named for him. Walk from Blackwell's Bookshop toward the church of St. Mary Magdalen, and in the center of Broad Street, just opposite Balliol College, lies a collection of white cobblestones that form a cross in the street to commemorate the spot where Archbishop Cranmer, Bishop Latimer, and Bishop Ridley were burned at the stake for the part they played in the reformation of the Church of England. Remnants of the old city wall still stand along the back side of Merton College, visible from Christ Church Meadow, and within the garden of New College, a reminder that King Charles I sought refuge within this fortified city during the English Civil War.

In this city in the fourteenth century, John Wycliffe translated the Bible into English and sent out his students, two by two, to preach the gospel. In this

Undergraduates are still met by the porters in the porter's lodge of their colleges when they first "go up" to Oxford. (Photo by Ben Dockery)

Above: "Freshers" dressed in "sub-fusk" (black suits, white shirt and tie, short gown, and Oxford cap) prepare to appear before the Vice Chancellor in the Sheldonian Theatre in the ceremony that makes them members of the university. (Photo by Rebecca Whitten Poe)

Opposite page: Down such a hole under a hedge in Christ Church Meadow, Alice followed a white rabbit to Wonderland one fine summer's day.

The "constabulary" of the university dressed in dark suits and bowler hats keep order on ceremonial occasions. Because of their skill in handling rowdy undergraduates in days gone by, they earned the name "Bull Dogs." (Photo by Rebecca Whitten Poe)

city Thomas Goodwin and John Owen, Puritan chaplains to Oliver Cromwell, headed Magdalen and Christ Church colleges during the Commonwealth. In this city George Whitfield, John Wesley, and Charles Wesley founded the Holy Club and began their personal pursuits of God that would blossom as the First Great Awakening.

In this city lived some of the most well-known characters of English literature. From Christ Church Meadow, Alice followed a rabbit down a hole into Wonderland. Along the banks of the Cherwell River, which flows into the Isis at Oxford, lived Ratty, Badger, Mole, and the wonderful Mr. Toad of Toad Hall. In this city, Harriet Vane finally accepted the marriage proposal of Lord Peter Wimsey, and here they married at St. Cross Church. One of Chaucer's springtime pilgrims to Canterbury set out

Jack and Warnie on vacation

(Used by permission of The Marion E. Wade Center, Wheaton College, Wheaton, IL.)

from Oxford. Here Inspector Morse kept the peace and Bertie Wooster's cousins Eustice and Claude frittered away their college years.

Oxford is a city that sets its own course, regardless of how the rest of the world goes. The River Thames flows below Oxford and above Oxford, but through the city flows the River Isis. The big bell in Tom Tower of Christ Church College tolls at five minutes past the hour according to Greenwich Mean Time because reason insists that Oxford is five minutes later than Greenwich. Even though Magdalen College pronounces its name *Maudlin*, St. Mary Magdalen Church pronounces its name the same way it would be pronounced anywhere else in the English-speaking world, except Cambridge of course, which also adds a final "e."

Oxford belongs to pedestrians, who stroll the narrow alley that leads from the High Street back to the secluded plaza of Oriel and Corpus Christi or the twisting passage that winds around from the Bridge of Sighs past the thirteenth-century Turf Tavern and out to Holywell Street. Pedestrians know the cobblestones that pave the college quads and the round river rocks that pave the yard around the Radcliffe Camera between St. Mary the Virgin Church and the Bodleian Library. Pedestrians notice the displays in the shop windows along the High Street and sculpted heads atop the gateposts outside the Sheldonian Theatre. Pedestrians have the time to glance up at the heads and creatures that ornament the buildings of Magdalen College or to peek in the college gates

Above: Keble College where Jack Lewis and Paddy Moore received their training as young officers before going to the front in 1917

Following page: Parson's Pleasure on the Cherwell River where Jack Lewis and Paddy Moore went with others to swim

while passing to catch a glimpse of the inevitable flowers and immaculate green turf that set off the privacy of a college quad. Pedestrians still throng the Cornmarket, now restricted to foot traffic only, where shoppers have gathered since an ox first forded the river.

The Oxford of pedestrians appears much as it has for centuries. The old bookshops, once as common as undergraduates, have almost all disappeared, replaced by souvenir shops and panini sandwich bars. The new tenants, however, inhabit the same centuries-old buildings, usually owned by one of the colleges, that the former tenants held. To see the real change that has overtaken Oxford, the pedestrian must leave the footpath and take the public transportation to pass the damage inflicted by the prosperity of the twentieth century. Before World War I, none of the damage had yet occurred, unless you believe Victorian architecture constitutes damage, and a reasonable argument could be made along those lines.

Still, after the aesthetic sacrilege that followed World War II, even Victorian architecture has gained a certain charm with the passage of time. The two most colossal relics of that era sit

The door to Janie Moore's flat at 58 Windmill Road

Above: Janie Moore's flat at 58 Windmill Road in Headington. Jack Lewis moved here in June 1921.

Opposite page: Janie Moore lived at 28 Warneford Road when she first moved to Oxford.

Jack Lewis read his winning English essay before the university from the rostrum in the Sheldonian Theatre.

Above: C. S. Lewis with the faculty of Magdalen College, Oxford

(Used by permission of The Marion E. Wade Center, Wheaton College, Wheaton, IL.)

Opposite page: In the graduation ceremony at Oxford University, candidates pass under this doorway of the Divinity School during the robing ceremony.

opposite one another on Parks Road, monuments to the complex and diverse opinions held in Oxford. Keble College, with its checkerboard neo-Gothic extravagance, was established in the second half of the nineteenth century as a home for the Oxford Movement, that high-church revival of spirituality within the Church of England that renewed the Christian faith for many in Victorian England. Across the street stands the University Museum, another neo-Gothic pile, constructed as a "cathedral to science," inspired by the Darwinian notion that God had become an obsolete hypothesis.

Everyone who has ever returned to Oxford after visiting her once realizes that they have their favorite spot, their favorite walk, their favorite college, and their favorite view of the dreaming spires. Some take the time to climb the Carfax Tower, the spire of St. Mary the Virgin, or the old Saxon Tower of St. Michael at the North Gate church. Others begin their return visit at the War Memorial Garden by the west gate to Christ Church Meadow in St. Aldate's Street. The bibliophiles make directly

Janie Moore's house at 76 Windmill Road in Headington

Above: Successful Oxford students receive their degrees before the vice chancellor, seated on his raised chair in the Sheldonian Theatre designed by Sir Christopher Wren.

Opposite page: Lewis became a fellow of Magdalen College in 1925.

for Blackwell's Bookshop, arguably the greatest bookstore in the world. The more robust reclaim the town by making the circuit on foot along the Cornmarket to the High Street, walking its length, past University College, Queen's College, and the Examination Schools, to Magdalen College, and then left along Longwall Street, skirting the remains of the old city wall incorporated into Magdalen, and turning left again at Holywell Street, past New College and the Holywell Music Hall, before opening onto Broad Street where Blackwell's faces the Clarendon Building, the old home of the university offices, and the Sheldonian Theatre, Sir Christopher Wren's first important commission and the location for all important university functions. Along the short stretch of Broad Street before reaching the Cornmarket again, the visitor passes Lincoln, Jesus, and Exeter colleges off a street to the left while Trinity and Balliol Colleges face Broad Street on the right. Photographs from a century ago reveal that not much has changed along these streets except the signs, the vehicles, and the clothing fashions.

A hundred years ago, however, Mr. Morris had not yet built his first little car in the garage in the back of what is now Regent's Park College in St. Giles. Not having built his first little car, he had not yet built the massive, sprawling motor-works factory at Cowley on the edge of Oxford. A hundred years ago, the sprawl of suburban estates had not yet blanketed the countryside leading out of town from Abingdon Road, Somerville Road, Woodstock Road, or the London Road. A hundred years ago, the world had not yet changed. A hundred years ago, the Union Jack flew over a global empire that comprised one sixth of the earth's land surface, while the Naval Jack flew over the fleet that dominated all of the earth's oceans. Oxford was the intellectual center of the empire where the next

generation of leaders in politics, commerce, science, and religion came for their final preparation before assuming the responsibilities of empire. Oxford was not simply a college town. Oxford was the university that set the standard for education in the world.

C. S. LEWIS AND HIS FRIENDS

Children born in the last years of the reign of Queen Victoria had grand-sounding names like Clive Staples Lewis and Warren Hamilton Lewis. These names would look handsome on a visiting card or on the nameplate of a barrister's office. They would sound most impressive when announced at a formal reception for members of Parliament. These names, however, sounded a bit daunting to two little boys growing up in a big house in the suburban hills outside Belfast, Northern Ireland, in the last years before Ireland's successful war for independence.

Daunting names were not to be tolerated; therefore, Clive Staples announced at the age of four that his name was Jacksie, which in time he shortened to Jack. For the next sixty years, those who loved him and knew him best called him Jack, while Clive Staples survived only as the initials *C. S.* on the title pages of the books he wrote. His older brother by three years could not be left to suffer with a name like Warren Hamilton, so Jack rechristened him Warnie, by which he would be called by his family and friends for seventy years. The title pages of his books also resorted to initials: *W. H.*

Individual friendships are difficult enough to explain, but how do we explain a circle of friends? Friendship is not like a business partnership that advances one's physical survival interests. Friends may advance one another's interests, but this comes as the result rather than as the cause of friendship. If anything, friendship detracts from the business of advancing one's own interests, but it suggests that people are more than a collection of chemicals and electro-neuron impulses.

A circle of friends with diverse backgrounds, personal aspirations, and emotional make-ups is a true wonder of nature. Friends are not like a hunting party or a work crew, which must perform a common task to insure survival.

Some people have a boundless capacity for friendship, while others have difficulty managing more than a few friends. Most people are indeed fortunate to have two or three good friends in the course of a life. C. S. Lewis accumulated friends the way other people accumulate pennies. Jack's first and closest friend throughout his life was his older brother, Warnie, who came to live in Oxford with him after twenty years' service in the army, during which time Warnie had become an alcoholic. He looked after Jack throughout their childhood until school separated them, but in adult life the roles reversed and Jack looked after Warnie.

Above: Owen Barfield in the 1920s

(Used by permission of The Marion E. Wade Center, Wheaton College, Wheaton, IL.)

Opposite page: The round Radcliffe Camera and the spire of St. Mary's across the fellows' garden of Exeter College where Tolkien, Dyson, and Coghill were undergraduates

Above: Exeter College faces narrow, medieval Turl Street that runs between Broad Street and the High Street.

Opposite page: The hall of Exeter College

After Warnie, Jack's friend of longest standing was a boy named Arthur Greeves from the neighborhood in Belfast. As a child, Jack had reluctantly agreed to meet Arthur after the insistence of his mother and went by to visit him one day when Arthur was sick in bed. Jack noticed a book of Norse tales lying on the bedside table. Their mutual interest in Norse mythology sparked a friendship that would last the rest of Jack's life. One of the marks of a true friendship is the remarkable quality of continuing in spite of separation, for Lewis left Northern Ireland for school, college, and life in England, while Greeves remained in Ireland. Much of what biographers know of the thoughts, attitudes, feelings, and private side of C. S. Lewis, however, is known because of the depths of himself that he poured out in his reams of letters to Greeves over the course of fifty years.

If Warnie and Greeves demonstrate Jack's long-term devotion to friendship, his friendship with Paddy Moore illustrates how quickly he could form friendships and just how seriously he took his friendships. Lewis and Moore met in Oxford in 1917, at the height of World War I. As a resident of Ireland, Lewis had no obligation to serve in the British Army. Nonetheless, he enlisted and began officer training with a battalion billeted at Keble College in Oxford. His roommate was Paddy Moore. Jack spent several weekends with Paddy in Bristol, with his mother Janie Moore, and Paddy's younger sister, Maureen. In those last, fading days of a world that would end forever with the devastation of the war, Lewis and Moore promised that if one of them should die in the war, the survivor would care for the other's family. Jack Lewis suffered a serious injury from shell fire in 1918, but Paddy Moore was killed. After the war, Jack Lewis went back to Oxford to complete his studies, but along with him went Janie and Maureen Moore. Mrs. Moore would live with Jack until her death in 1951.

When Jack Lewis returned to Oxford after World War I, he came as a thoroughgoing atheist. The slaughter of the war merely capped a conclusion he had reached about God following the death of his mother from cancer when he was only nine years old. Lewis met many other young veterans like himself alongside the younger group of undergraduates who had not fought in the war and took a more frivolous approach to life. Having decided that he wanted to earn distinction as a poet and pursue an academic career, Lewis had the combined pressure of doing well enough with his studies to gain notice *and* of providing for Mrs. Moore and Maureen out of the allowance his father provided. Lewis wanted a position teaching philosophy, but when none was offered him at the completion of his studies, he stayed on and completed another course of study in English literature. He won the Chancellor's English Essay prize in 1921 and read his winning essay from the rostrum in the Sheldonian Theatre before the University. Finally, in 1925 Lewis received an appointment as a fellow of Magdalen College, where he would spend almost thirty years tutoring pupils in literature.

The pressures of domestic and academic life would seem to leave little extra time for friendships to develop, but Lewis made his new friends among those who shared his interests. Lewis made friends with Nevill Coghill, another Irishman reading the English course, who shared Jack's enthusiasm for long, energetic walks in the country. Owen Barfield shared Lewis's love of poetry and his disdain for the modern trends in poetry. Upon finishing their courses of study, Coghill was awarded a fellowship at Exeter College and Lewis at Magdalen College, but Barfield tried to earn his living by writing before finally turning to law and a lifetime in his father's law practice. During this period, Lewis had been writing an ambitiously long narrative poem entitled *Dymer*. When he asked Nevill Coghill's opinion of his poem, Coghill liked it so much that he passed it on to a friend who worked at the publishing house J. M. Dent, which published the poem as a book in 1926.

In 1926 John Ronald Reuel Tolkien, the new Professor of Anglo-Saxon and fellow of Pembroke College, started a new club for the pleasure of members of the faculty who wanted to read the Icelandic sagas and myths in the Old Icelandic language. Coghill added his name as a cofounder, and C. S. Lewis soon joined as well, though neither of them could read Old Icelandic. This club, known as the Kolbitars, met regularly during the

Above: The interior of the chapel of Exeter College
Opposite page: The chapel of Exeter College is modeled on St. Chappell in Paris.

The vaulted ceiling of the chapel of Exeter College

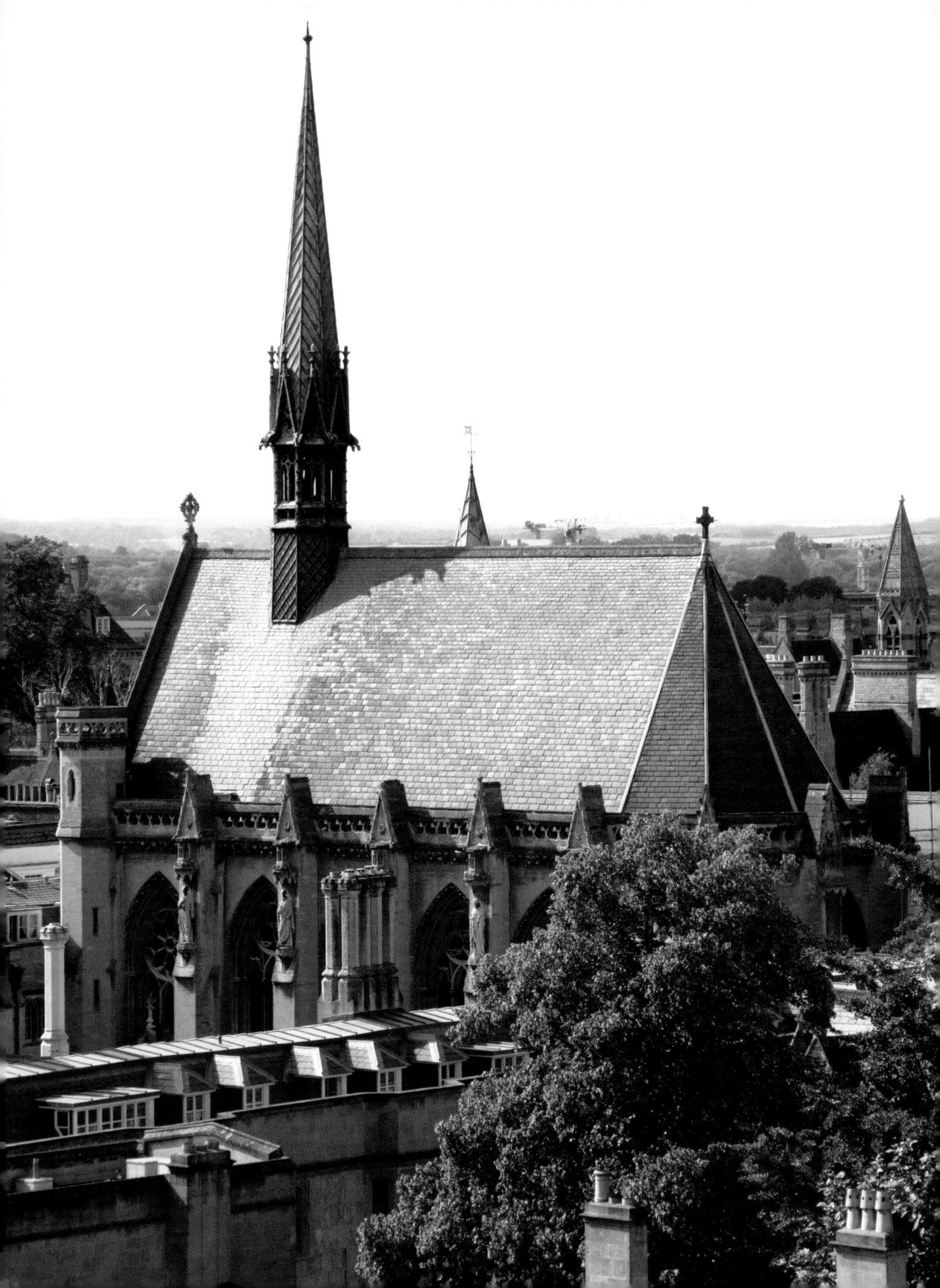

Above: The great hall at Christ Church College, where Lord David Cecil was an undergraduate viewed from the War Memorial Garden in memory of those who died during World War I

Opposite page: The spire of the chapel of Exeter College

eight-week terms, and Lewis eventually learned through these gatherings that Tolkien loved the old Norse myths as much as he did.

Though Lewis had the capacity for immediate friendships, he found Tolkien more of an acquired taste. Their first meeting had taken place at an English faculty tea, but no great friendship formed then. Shortly afterward, Tolkien shook up the entire English faculty by proposing a revision to "the syllabus," the scope of what students studied in their undergraduate program of study. Tolkien proposed placing an emphasis on the medieval language and its texts with only minor glimpses at "modern writers," by which he meant Chaucer, Spencer, and the popular entertainer William Shakespeare. The opponents of this proposal favored the study of English literature on a much broader scale up to the present day. Tolkien's compromise proposal placed an ending date for the syllabus at 1830.

The study of English literature has become such a standard feature of education that it is hard to believe that it was still a newcomer to Oxford University in the 1920s. It had only been taught as a course of study since the late nineteenth century, and not everyone was sure it had the rigor needed for university study. After all, undergraduates read

The hall at Magdalen College where Jack Lewis ate his meals with the rest of the college during term

Dickens and Thackeray for their own amusement. They went to Shakespeare's plays for an evening's entertainment. What more could they do? Tolkien argued that the study of medieval English language and literature would add all the rigor anyone would possibly want, and it would spare him from teaching modern writers who did not interest him in the least. Tolkien won Lewis over, and the two of them joined in the academic battle that ended with Tolkien's victory in 1931.

Between doing battle together on behalf of medieval English and reading Icelandic sagas, Lewis and Tolkien developed a strong friendship. Their common love of what Lewis called "Northerness" provided the cement. If possible, Tolkien's love for the Norse myths exceeded even that of Lewis. While Lewis labored to gain fame as a great poet, Tolkien labored privately on an enterprise all his own that he never expected anyone ever to see. For several years before meeting Lewis, Tolkien had been at work creating an entire world with its own mythology and tales.

Tolkien had only shown his work to one person, a former schoolmaster who severely criticized it, before he finally showed it to Lewis in December 1929. Lewis could not have been more enthusiastic in his praise for what would eventually be named *The Silmarillion*. Years later, Tolkien wrote that what Lewis had given him early on was the encouragement to think that what he was doing was worthwhile. Lewis enjoyed hearing Tolkien read his work aloud; so began a practice that would continue to grow for many years.

Another important event occurred in 1929 that would influence the growing circle of relationships in Oxford. Albert Lewis, Jack and War-

The cloisters of Magdalen College

The New Building at Magdalen College viewed from Addison's Walk

nie's father, died in Belfast. While Warnie looked forward to completing his time of service in the army with retirement pay, he needed a place to live. The brothers decided to sell the house in Belfast and buy a house in Oxford where Warnie could live with Jack and Janie and Maureen Moore. In 1930 they bought a house and eight acres at the edge of Shotover Hill, an ancient and well-known landmark near the London Road in Headington. The house was named the Kilns in recognition of two old imposing brick kilns that remained on the property from the time when it had been a brickyard. In 1932 Warnie retired from the army and moved into the house that would be his home for more than forty years.

Also in 1930 Nevill Coghill introduced Lewis to another literary man, Henry Victor Dyson, who was known to his friends as Hugo. Dyson had been at Exeter with Coghill and went off to lecture in English literature at Reading University after finishing his studies at Oxford. In their letters and diaries, Dyson's friends described him as witty, exuberant, noisy, and amusing. He was energetic and tended to burst, or perhaps explode, into a room, setting everything and everyone awhirl. Hugo Dyson immediately appealed to the two Lewis brothers, who always enjoyed his company when he came up to Oxford for relief from the normalcy and ordinariness of life at his "red brick school."

The Question of God

Owen Barfield said that he himself believed in evolution but never changed at all. On the other hand, he said that Jack Lewis did not believe in evolution and was constantly changing.[1] Through his conversations and interactions with his new friends at Oxford, Lewis had gradually changed his mind about God. Perhaps he had been hasty. Perhaps he had been immature. One thing, however, had become clear to Lewis: he could not ignore certain inescapable aspects of his own experience that conflicted with his atheism.

Since childhood, Lewis had noticed that certain experiences stirred within him a feeling, or sensation or something else, he could not quite describe or locate, which he would eventually label "Joy." That feeling, if that's what it was, came upon him unexpectedly. It was not something he could seek, work up, or hold onto even when it did come. It was a feeling that evoked longing and desire for something not known more than it was a feeling that conveyed a sense of satisfaction or fulfillment. As a young boy he had first experienced it upon seeing a miniature garden that his brother had fashioned in the lid of a tin cookie box. Lewis described it as his first experience of

Above: The Kilns in Headington where Jack and Warnie Lewis lived from 1930 until their deaths

Opposite page: The Tolkiens lived at 22 Northmoor Road in North Oxford from 1925 until 1930.

Above: Jack Lewis stood his scholarship examination in the hall of Oriel College.

Opposite page: The gate to Pembroke College where Tolkien held his professorship from 1925 until 1945

beauty. The memory of this experience was as vivid to him more than fifty years later as it had been when it first occurred, and the memory became a touchstone by which he compared later experiences.

The experience came upon him again through Beatrix Potter's little book *Squirrel Nutkin*. The longing and the dissatisfaction came upon him again as what he could only call "the idea of Autumn." The sensation troubled him, yet he wanted to reawaken it. Somehow it seemed to make him aware of something "quite different from ordinary life."

His third experience came while flipping through the pages of a book and coming upon *Tegner's Drapa*. His eyes fell on the passage:

> *I heard a voice that cried,*
> *Balder the beautiful*
> *Is dead, is dead –* [2]

Without knowing who Balder was, Lewis felt himself moved powerfully far away into another region – remote, cold, spacious, severe. As in the other cases, the feeling left as quickly as it had come. Yet it remained a permanent aspect of his memory, just as

Lewis spent his first night in Oxford at a boarding house on Mansfield Road between Holywell and Jewett.

Lewis won a scholarship to University College in 1917 at the height of World War I.

we remember a cut or a burn but lose the feeling. We only remember that we had the feeling. We recognize it when we have the same feeling again, but our memory cannot reawaken the feeling. Only the cause of the feeling can do that.

Lewis came to associate the feeling with Norse mythology and Northerness. It became the original point in common with Arthur Greeves and with Tolkien. When he discovered Wagnerian music and Arthur Rackham's illustrations to *Siegfried and the Twilight of the Gods*, Lewis bathed himself in these aids to Northerness, hoping, through them, to recapture that experience he so vividly recalled. Though they did not re-create the experience, they reminded him that the experience had really happened, not just once, but several times.

As he grew older, the fascination with the Norse mythologies turned into a more detached, intellectual interest. Pleasure changed to a scholar's study, and the fire grew cold. Lewis had a string of disastrous and painful experiences in the public schools where he had been incarcerated for his education. At last his father commuted his sentence and sent him off to Surrey to live with a private tutor. In place of the romantic imagination that Lewis had cultivated for so long, he discovered a new way of thought and conversation rooted in pure logic. His tutor, W. T. Kirkpatrick, had grown up a Presbyterian but had adopted atheist views, which gave Lewis "fresh ammunition" for his own views now that he had taken up logical argument and disputation as his new recreation. With Kirkpatrick, Lewis read Homer, Demosthenes, Cicero, Lucretius, Catullus, Tacitus,

The front quad of University College where Jack Lewis spent his undergraduate years.

Heroditus, Virgil, Euripedes, Sophocles, and Aeschylus. He read Greek and Latin to prepare for the scholarship examination that would result in his election to University College. In those days before radio and television when motion pictures were in their infancy, Lewis read for fun and amusement like everyone else. If the Greek and Latin classics were his work, then Milton, Spenser, Malory, and Morris were his play.

Lewis discovered pleasures along the way, but in discovering pleasures, he also discovered that they were not that for which he longed. Sexual experience belonged to an entirely different order than that which he called Joy. In the meantime, he had managed to compartmentalize his intellect and his imagination. Looking back on that time, Lewis would observe, "Nearly all that I loved I believed to be imaginary; nearly all that I believed to be real I thought grim and meaningless."[3] He could not escape the beauty of nature, but he could not reconcile beauty with the pain and evil that he found in nature. At that point, however, he was willing to take the pain, meaninglessness, and brevity of existence in exchange for not having to deal with a God who might interfere with his independence.

Then, while Lewis saw himself as a confirmed materialist, he read the poetry of Yeats, who somehow seemed to think that another world of spirits might lie alongside our world and that some point of contact might be made between the two. In short, Lewis came face-to-face with the idea of Magic. He did not pursue it, but he wondered. In that state of mind, he first came across George MacDonald's *Phantastes*. This book

The highly decorated vaulted ceiling of the gate house of University College

Logic Lane provides pedestrians with a shortcut through the precincts of University College.

roused in Lewis all that seemed to elude him, but now he felt that it eluded him not because he could not reach it, but because he was busy doing something that stood in the way of his reaching it. He was the barrier to what was always there but always out of reach.

Lewis's first experience of Oxford came when he arrived one winter's day in 1916 to sit for his scholarship examination, which was administered in the Hall of Oriel College. While snow fell outside, the Hall was dreadfully cold, and all the examinees wrote while wearing coats, scarves, and gloves. He won his scholarship and went up to Oxford in the summer term of 1917 as a member of University College. After the summer term, however, he entered the University Officer's Training Corps, where he met Paddy Moore. By November, on his nineteenth birthday, he was at the front line. During the winter, he contracted "trench fever" and was sent to hospital for three weeks' recovery. During this illness he first read G. K. Chesterton's essays on Christianity. Lewis read Chesterton because he liked the way Chesterton wrote, not because of his views. Chesterton's humor and goodness in the context of impeccable logic had a profound impact on Lewis, who later observed, "A young man who wishes to remain a sound Atheist cannot be too careful of his reading."[4]

Lewis grew up quickly in the war. He met the World and its Nonsense. He was severely wounded by a British shell and found himself contemplating his own death. On reflection he realized, "I had proved that there was a fully conscious 'I' whose connections with the 'me' of introspection were loose and transitory."[5] From this experience he gained a new appreciation for the "energy, fertility, and urgency; the resources, the triumphs, and even the insolence, of things that grow."[6] Perhaps life was more precious than a good materialist cared to admit.

After the war, Lewis returned to Oxford, where he met Barfield. Lewis found that he and Barfield shared all the same interests but disagreed with each other about almost everything. For several years Lewis was swept up with himself as a man of good sense. With this "new look" Lewis simply categorized his deep experience of Joy as mere "aesthetic experience." About this time, however, Barfield and another new friend, A. C. Harwood, embraced the teachings of Rudolf Steiner and became anthroposophists. Lewis was horrified. His friends had accepted the reality of an entire spiritual world and notions of afterlife and preexistence.

The ensuing dispute between Lewis and Barfield had an unintended result. Barfield did not persuade Lewis of the truth of anthroposophism, but he did destroy two of Lewis's intellectual props. First, Lewis had to give up the uncritical assumption that old ideas that have gone out of fashion are always wrong and that the current fashion is always right. The current fashion will soon be just another old fashion. The ideas themselves must be evaluated before they are dismissed out of hand for being old. Second, Lewis had to give up his old view that only the physical world of sense experience exists, simply because sensory experience cannot lead to this conclusion. Sensory experience can only go far enough to say that it only gives knowledge of the physical world. It cannot give data about the possibility of other worlds. It is limited in what it can tell us. Lewis realized that the reliability of rational thought, the concept of moral judgment, and the experience of beauty all go beyond mere sensory experience and point to some other reality than just the physical. Lewis had to admit to himself that there appeared to be some sort of "Mind" behind the universe.

While riding up Headington Hill on a bus, Jack Lewis concluded that there must be a God.

Jack Lewis experienced no blinding lights or burning bushes when he finally accepted the existence of God as one of those inconvenient facts of life, like flu or income taxes. He did not like this new fact, but at least the God he believed existed was the kind who keeps his distance and minds his own business. This change of mind for Lewis was not exactly a mountain-top experience either. It did not take place in a sacred grove or at one of the many holy spots in Oxford. It happened as the bus on which he rode lumbered jauntily up Headington Hill on his way home for the day from Oxford. He had simply reached a conclusion that his logically trained philosophical mind could not avoid any longer. Lewis did not have *faith* in the God that he believed existed any more than a blind man has faith in light. On the basis of the evidence, a blind man may conclude that something people call light must exist, but he has only the vaguest notion what it is. Even more, he literally does not see what it has to do with him.

Jack Lewis lived with Janie Moore and her daughter Maureen at Hillsboro House on the Western Road (now 14 Holyoake) in Headington from 1922 until 1930.

By the summer of 1929, however, Lewis had a clearer understanding of what or who God must be. For one thing, he does *not* keep his distance or mind his own business. He realized that he had come into the presence of deity, though not yet face-to-face. Perhaps his training in medieval and classical literature had prepared him for what to do now. Perhaps his recollections from childhood prepared him. Perhaps the simple fact of finding himself in this position left Lewis with no other conceivable option. He knelt and prayed to the God who made him.

Not yet a Christian, but a theist, Lewis decided to do the honorable thing and go to church, but he did not see what Jesus had to do with anything. A certain amount of philosophy and reason can carry a person just so far, but the "God" of Plato and the other philosophers is a far cry from the God of the Bible, and Lewis's God was still a far cry from the God who entered the world in human flesh. Lewis could not see the point of God coming into the world, much less dying on a cross and rising from the dead.

Where philosophy and reason could not take him, Lewis discovered that imagination and language easily could. Imagination goes beyond the mere concrete and analytical world of philosophy, no matter how speculative the philosophy may be. Philosophy is tied to the physical world even when

Addison's Walk at Magdalen College where Jack Lewis talked with Tolkien and Dyson about Christianity and myth

it ponders the world of ideals. Imagination, on the other hand, journeys beyond the physical world and comes back again. Every great scientific breakthrough has come not from building on old, established understandings of science and reasoning, from there to something radically different. Instead, people like Einstein take flight through imagination, which takes them somewhere else and returns them with a new understanding of the world.

For years Lewis had been fascinated by the stories of imagination that emerged in every ancient culture. He loved the mythologies. One night in mid-September 1931, Lewis invited Tolkien and Dyson to dine with him at Magdalen College. After dinner, they took an evening stroll in the expansive grounds of Magdalen along Addison's Walk. This footpath makes a circle through the woods around a large meadow on an island formed by the Cherwell River and several small tributaries. As they walked through the shadows under the arches of ancient trees, the conversation turned to talk of metaphor and myth. Lewis wrote to his friend Arthur Greeves that the discussion was "interrupted by a rush of wind which came suddenly on the still, warm evening and sent so many leaves pattering down that we thought it was raining. We all held our breath...."[7]

As they talked, Tolkien and Dyson helped Lewis see something about himself and about the meaning of God coming into the world to die sacrificially for those he loved. Whenever Lewis encountered the idea of sacrificial death in any of the mythologies of the ancient world, he liked it very much. When he read of a god who sacrificed himself to himself, he was "mysteriously moved."[8] He delighted in the stories of gods who died and then lived again, whether Balder of the Norse or Adonis of the Greeks. He liked these stories anywhere he found them, *except* in the Gospels.

Lewis said that he did not see the point of the death and resurrection of Jesus, because it all seemed like just another version of the universal story of a dying and rising god. Tolkien replied that the story of Jesus is like all the other stories, with one tremendous difference: "It really happened."[9] The idea of a true myth hit Lewis like lightning. It also provided Lewis with an explanation of why this same story of the dying and rising god would be found in cultures all over the world. The God who had tracked him down had prepared every culture to receive the true story by planting the poetic myth that Jesus fulfilled.

The friends talked until 3:00 in the morning when Tolkien finally left to go home. Dyson and Lewis sat up another hour before they finally went to bed. A little over a week passed during which all of this talk brewed in Lewis's brain. On Monday, September 28, 1931, Warnie took Jack for a ride in his motorcycle to the Whipsnade Zoo. Jack rode in a sidecar. Years later Jack wrote,

> When we set out I did not believe that Jesus Christ is the Son of God, and when we reached the zoo I did. Yet I had not exactly spent the journey in thought. Nor in great emotion. "Emotional" is perhaps the last word we can apply to some of the most important events. It was more like when a man, after long sleep, still lying motionless in bed, becomes aware that he is now awake.[10]

Magdalen Tower

TWO

AN AGE OF SOCIETIES AND CLUBS

When C. S. Lewis went to Magdalen College as a fellow in English, he was surprised to find that Magdalen had no undergraduate societies. As an undergraduate at University College, Lewis had enjoyed the familiarity and sociability that college clubs offered. Unlike the American system of Greek letter fraternities and sororities, the college societies came and went, forming around common interests of students for a time. At University College Lewis served as secretary of the Martlets, a literary club restricted to twelve members that imagined for itself an ancient lineage stretching back three hundred years. In fact, the club had its beginnings in 1892.[11]

Open windows on the quad provide light for the medieval cloisters of Magdalen College.

Lewis learned that Magdalen did not simply *not* have student societies. A previous president had outlawed student societies because they tended to be "savagely exclusive clubs of rich dipsomaniacs."[12] Lewis reasoned that the prohibition might have produced a more decent college, but at the expense of its intellectual life. He set about to change the situation, which required some political maneuvering in order to gain the support of the

Opposite page: Magdalen Tower rising above the hall as viewed from the cloisters.

Above: Fellows continue to give guidance to students when they first come up to Oxford. (Photo by Rebecca Whitten Poe)

Below: Some of the smooth river stone streets of Oxford appear as they did 700 years ago. (Photo by Ben Dockery)

other fellows about a relaxation of the rules. He started by inviting a few students to his room in order to read Elizabethan plays on Monday evenings. On Wednesday evenings he invited students to his room to read Anglo-Saxon. This reading group came to be called the "Beer and Beowulf Evenings" because it tended to move from reading to talk around the fire over beer.[13] By this means, Lewis gradually instilled in students the idea of forming groups of their own around matters of common interest but, preferably for Lewis, matters of common intellectual interest. By 1928 he had succeeded in his subterfuge to the extent that the students founded the Michaelmas Club.

During his early days as a fellow of Magdalen College, Lewis did not neglect his own need for friendship and meaningful conversation. Besides enjoying the company of Tolkien and the other members of the Kolbitars each fortnight during term to read Old Icelandic, he also attended a fortnightly philosophical supper presided over by William Francis Ross Hardie, Fellow and Tutor in Philosophy at Corpus Christi College.[14] In 1939 he met one evening a week to read Dante with Colin Hardie while taking part in a discussion group every Monday at tea with the Magdalen chaplain Adam Fox and a group of "pious undergraduates."[15] In 1940, Lewis wrote to Warnie about a meeting of the Gibbon Club. Being with people one enjoyed, who liked the same things one liked, formed the only good basis for friendship, as Lewis would reflect years later when he wrote *The Four Loves*. These gatherings were not organizations, but occasions for friendship.

Almost anything could be an excuse to form a new club. The Oyster Club celebrated the conclusion of the tedious grading of examinations each year.[16] At Oxford, students are not subjected to continuous evaluation by tests throughout their university career. They write papers for their tutors each week, which they read aloud to their teacher, who comments on the paper as it is read. They only have two tests – one their first year in order to stay and one at the end of their time at Oxford. The entire success or failure of the students depends upon the outcome of this second, days-long examination in which they are expected to know everything. Students convene in the great Examination Schools Building, where they sit their exams under watchful eyes. This one test explains why Oxford has one of the highest suicide rates in the world. After the students have done their best, however, the fellows must grade the examinations and decide the outcome of the students' Oxford careers. The Oyster Club celebrated the relief of finishing grading by eating oysters.

Tolkien also enjoyed these gatherings of likeminded people. As early as his days at King Edward's School in Birmingham, Tolkien and three of his friends called themselves the Tea Club, or T.C., because they found ways to make tea in the school library and were clever enough to hide their daring. During summer term, they had tea at Barrow's Store, so they changed their name to the Barrovian Society, or B.S. In the end, they combined it all and called themselves by their grand initials: T.C.B.S.[17] All four of the friends went to war, but only Tolkien and Christopher Wiseman returned. After the war these two found they no longer had anything in common. The enormity of the dreadfulness of the Great War cannot be overstated. Tolkien went as a second lieutenant in B Company of the 13th Battalion of the Lancashire Fusiliers. He survived the Battle of the Somme in 1916 only to contract "trench fever," which was so severe that he was finally removed to England to recover.

After the war, when he returned to Oxford with his young family, Tolkien had hopes of finding a teaching position at a college. Instead he secured a small job working on the *New English Dictionary* and supplemented his meager salary by taking pupils from some of the colleges that were short of tutors. The Tolkiens lived in a flat at 1 Alfred Street (now Pusey Street). Tolkien had already begun to write his great mythology that would eventually include the tale that became the Lord of the Rings. He read his tale "The Fall of Gondolin" to the Essay Club of Exeter College, an undergraduate society that included Nevill Coghill and Hugo Dyson, both of whom would also become members of the Inklings.[18]

A group, which included Lewis, with more ideological overtones developed in the early 1930s around Tolkien, at the time of his proposed revision of the English syllabus. Its members called this gathering the Cave, and they met for informal dinners. They continued to meet after their success with the syllabus, well into the 1940s. Reflecting on their success in a letter to his brother, Jack said that his "party" in English School politics had managed to move from their rebellious role as the anti-junto group to the status as the new junto, and he wondered,

A relief above the doorway of the Examination Schools Building offers hope to the candidates about to stand their examinations that at least some students receive their degrees.

Above: This relief above the doorway of the Examination Schools Building depicts an undergraduate in his short gown facing an examination from three fellows of the university.

Opposite page: The Examination Schools Building where undergraduates take the dreaded examinations for their degrees contains the largest lecture halls of the university. Here Jack Lewis held forth with his lectures on Medieval and Renaissance literature to standing-room-only crowds.

Above: The Tolkiens lived at 1 Alfred Street (now Pusey Street) when they first came to Oxford after World War I.

Below: Jack Lewis had rooms on what Americans call the second floor and what the English call the first floor of the New Building. His two windows lie just above the wisteria vines to the right of the central façade.

"How long will it take us to become corrupt in our turn?"[19] The Cave dinners appear to have been a time of frolic, laughter, and choice poetry rather than deep conversation. In the days of triumph, the Cave must have involved a large number of the English faculty. Jack enjoyed one gathering of the Cave at Balliol College in December 1939 at which Maurice Roy Ridley read from Swinburne, because it was "more frolic and youthful" than they had experienced in many years.[20] A few months later, however, he remarked in disappointment that only Herbert Francis Brett-Smith and Leonard Rice-Oxley had joined him, Tolkien, and Dyson for the Cave. Of course, Dyson was still a lecturer at Reading at the time and not yet a member of the English faculty at Oxford. Coghill rarely attended the Cave anymore.[21]

It was an age of great literary circles, but not one of the future members of the Inklings set out to form a great literary circle. They were simply friends who enjoyed each other's company. A few years earlier another famous literary group had formed in London. The Bloomsbury Group included writers like Lytton Strachey, E. M. Forster, and Virginia Woolf and her husband, Leonard. The members of this group lived in and around the Bloomsbury district of London before and after World War I. In New York a group that came to be called the Algonquin Round Table met for lunch every day at the Algonquin Hotel. Dorothy Parker reigned as queen of this group that continued for more than a decade after World War I until the Depression scattered its members. In Nashville, the Fugitive Poets formed around John Crow Ransom at Vanderbilt during and following World War I. In a slower, less complicated world, the gathering of friends for literary conversation in general, and discussion of what they were writing in particular, occurred in great cities and remote provinces, including the group in Charleston that met with Dubose Heyward and Josephine Pinkney and the group in Oxford that met with C. S. Lewis and J. R. R. Tolkien.

The doorway to the staircase that leads to Lewis's rooms above the ground level arcade of the New Building

THE BEGINNINGS OF THE INKLINGS

Perhaps it was inevitable that something like the Inklings would eventually form. In fact, the group began as another undergraduate society. The actual founder was an undergraduate at University College named Edward Tangye-Lean, who wanted a literary group whose members would read their compositions and receive criticism from the others. Tolkien and Lewis, who was Tangye-Lean's tutor, agreed to take part. Tolkien remarked that the group soon died, but that he and Lewis survived. Lewis appropriated from

After his conversion, Jack Lewis attended morning prayer in the chapel of Magdalen College every day in term.

Above: The daily ritual of college life brought Jack Lewis through the cloisters to attend chapel and to dine in the hall.

Opposite page: After attending the inaugural lecture of Adam Fox as Professor of Poetry at the Divinity School, Jack Lewis described it as "the most beautiful room in Oxford."

the students the name for the circle of friends who had begun to gather in his rooms at Magdalen College. Tolkien said that the name was a jest because it suggested "people with vague or half-formed intimations and ideas plus those who dabble in ink."[22]

Because the Inklings were friends rather than a formal organization or club, they kept no minutes and elected no officers. They always ran the danger of becoming what Lewis called "the inner ring," that cliquish group of insiders who exalted themselves at the expense of those they excluded. Several factors saved them from this fate. First, they all had many interests and other friends. Second, they always tended to invite other people to "come along" for an evening. Most importantly, as Humphrey Carpenter observed, the Inklings were held together by friendship rather than any desire for power.[23] On one occasion, however, the exercise of power might have seemed the object of the group. It all began as a joke over breakfast.

In 1938, some senior members of the university nominated Sir Edmund Chambers for the Professor of Poetry. When Adam Fox, who was one of the Inklings, heard at breakfast one morning of Chambers' nomination, he declared, "This is simply shocking. They might as well make me professor."[24] Jack Lewis immediately responded, "Right, we will" and set about orchestrating the campaign to elect Fox to the post.

An elderly academic, Chambers approached poetry as a scholar whose lectures had a reputation for dullness. Fox, the chaplain, had no academic qualification for the post, but he had published a book-length poem with a simple flavor called *Old King Coel* in 1937. The Inklings rallied around Fox and argued for the importance of having a practicing poet as the Professor of Poetry. The election of Fox amounted to a great coup for Lewis, Tolkien, Dyson, and Coghill, but in the cold light of day, Lewis reflected that Fox might not prove to be all he had hoped for in a Professor of Poetry, who was expected to lecture on poetry. Instead of the great, new things about poetry that Lewis expected from one of his circle, the inaugural address of the new professor given in the venerable Divinity School adjacent to the Bodleian Library was "very good but not capital."[25]

For all his years in Oxford, Fox's lecture was the first occasion on which Lewis ever entered the Divinity School. In describing the experience in a letter to his brother Warnie, Lewis said, "This is simply the most beautiful room in Oxford or perhaps in England – all stone, perpendicular, with a most choice roof – all very white set off with almost black unpolished oak for railings and benches."[26]

In the end, however, Lewis felt justified in his campaign for Fox when Chambers delivered the Sydney Lee Lecture in February 1940. In a letter to Warnie, Lewis wrote of Chambers' lecture that he "was so portentously dull that I think even his own supporters must have been ashamed of him."[27]

Though the Inklings ostensibly met to read their own work, they were not restricted in their interests to literature. Most of them had a deep appreciation for music, especially Warnie, who took up playing the piano after his retirement from the army. They frequently attended concerts in Oxford at the Holywell

Above: The Lewis brothers loved music and frequently attended concerts at the Holywell Music Room.

Opposite page: The Sheldonian Theatre viewed through the lacy windows of the Divinity School.

The interior space of the Holywell Music Room which the Lewis brothers so loved offers an intimate and acoustically superb setting for recitals and chamber concerts.

Above: Nevill Coghill used to say that he knew a concert would be good if he saw Warnie Lewis in the audience. Oxford still abounds with evening concerts such as this performance by the Oxford City Orchestra in the Sheldonian Theatre.

Opposite page: Lewis and Tolkien met together at the Eastgate Hotel on Monday mornings.

A formal photo of Charles Williams, for use on the jackets of his books.

(Used by permission of The Marion E. Wade Center, Wheaton College, Wheaton, IL.)

Music Room. They made trips to London for the music, especially for the Wagnerian operas.

Without minutes or other records, we do not know any details of what happened at a gathering of the Inklings in the early days. Nonetheless, a good deal can be inferred in the same way that Jesus described the activity of the Holy Spirit by analogy with the wind: "The wind blows wherever it pleases. You hear its sound, but you cannot tell where it comes from or where it is going" (John 3:8). We can see the tremendous effect of the mutual encouragement that the Inklings provided to one another during the 1930s. Not until 1936 do we have any documentary evidence that such a group as the Inklings existed when Lewis first wrote to Charles Williams to express his appreciation for *Place of the Lion* and to invite him to meet with him, Nevill Coghill, Tolkien, Warnie, and their "informal club called the Inklings."[28] In 1937 Lewis wrote again to Charles Williams to invite him to attend a meeting of the Inklings on October 20 or 27 when he would be reading from his new

The Inklings met every Tuesday morning for many years at the Eagle and Child in St. Giles.

C. S. Lewis and an unidentified friend at a pub

(Used by permission of The Marion E. Wade Center, Wheaton College, Wheaton, IL.)

"thriller about a journey to Mars."[29] In 1938 Tolkien mentioned in a letter to Stanley Unwin, his publisher, that C. S. Lewis had read the manuscript of *Out of the Silent Planet* "aloud to our local club (which goes in for reading things short and long aloud)."[30] Later the same year, in another letter to Unwin, Tolkien mentioned that he and Lewis had nominated Adam Fox, another member of their "literary club," to the post of Professor of Poetry, and Fox had won the election.[31] Tolkien also mentioned that he had read *The Hobbit* to this group before adding, "We are slowly getting even into print." They were helping one another become better writers while encouraging each other to persevere.

In a letter from Lewis to Warnie on November 11, 1939, at the beginning of World War II, we find the Inklings mentioned with an indication of its regular attendees. In addition to Jack and Warnie Lewis, mention is made of Nevill Coghill, Hugo Dyson, Tolkien, and Charles Williams. Lewis mentions that Tolkien read a selection from his "new Hobbit" while Lewis read some of his new book on the "Problem of Pain."[32] The new Hobbit is the Lord of the Rings, which did not yet have a title.

The friends had settled into a routine of meeting in Lewis's rooms in Magdalen College every Thursday evening after dinner. *Dinner* at Oxford colleges included coffee and conversation afterward, so that the Inklings did not begin to convene until after 9:30 p.m. at the earliest and could go on until 1:00 a.m. without difficulty. In addition to the evening gatherings, Lewis and Tolkien had begun the habit of meeting at the Eastgate Hotel on Monday mornings when neither had tutorial duties.[33] On Tuesday mornings the other Inklings who could make it gathered at the Eagle and Child, a small pub in St. Giles often referred to as the Bird and Baby.

The original sign of the Eagle and Child as the Inklings knew it was removed during renovations and replaced by an oval sign. Walter Hooper rescued the old sign and presented it to the C. S. Lewis Foundation for preservation at the Kilns.

(Photo by Rebecca Whitten Poe)

Above: The Inklings often went to the Mitre for supper.

Opposite page: Nevill Coghill walked along the narrow and ever narrowing Turl Street as he made his way from Exeter College to the High Street and a meal at the Mitre.

Throughout the 1930s, the friends continued to entertain each other with a remarkable and varied collection of what they were writing, from scholarly articles and books, to poetry, to fantasy, to science fiction. Within this circle, as previously mentioned, Tolkien found the encouragement to keep working on his mythological world that included *The Silmarillion*, *The Hobbit*, and the beginning of the Lord of the Rings. Lewis had been hard at work on his first important work as a scholar, *The Allegory of Love*. In 1933 his conversion had spurred him to write an allegorical account of his conversion along the lines of Bunyan's *The Pilgrim's Progress*, which he named *The Pilgrim's Regress*. Soon after the publication of *The Allegory of Love* in 1936, Lewis wrote his first science fiction novel, *Out of the Silent Planet*, which was published in 1938. Along the way, most of the Inklings were writing and publishing poetry.

THE DARK SHADOW

In both *The Hobbit* and *The Pilgrim's Regress*, which were products of the first half of the 1930s when the Depression spread its shadow across the world, Lewis and Tolkien wrote about the internal battles that everyone faces in some way or other. The inner conflicts and moments of darkness create the stories that play out as journeys. They

Above: Jack Lewis chose for his bedroom the little end room in the attic, reminiscent of the favorite room of Jack and Warnie in the house of their childhood. (Photo by Ben Dockery)

Previous page: The Tolkiens found their house on Northmoor Road too small, so they moved next door to number 20 where they lived from 1930 until 1947. Here Tolkien would write most of the Lord of the Rings.

would go on to write about the cosmic problem of evil in later books, but they only had a basis for exploring cosmic evil in the Lord of the Rings and the Chronicles of Narnia because they understood that the problem of evil comes from the creative imagination of people. People, rather than God, are the authors of evil. To destroy evil, God can destroy people, enslave people so that they cannot do evil, or change people so that they desire not to do evil.

Tolkien's Bilbo in *The Hobbit* struggles with a fear that cripples him and prevents him from being free to be himself. Lewis's John in *The Pilgrim's Regress* has a thousand demons that hold him captive, for he is captivated by a host of rival ideas. Neither Bilbo nor John can be freed from the shadows that hang over them until they admit the darkness that they have nurtured and cher-

The pond at the Kilns formed in the hole from which clay had been dug to make bricks. Lewis loved to swim and punt in his pond.

Among the many landscaping improvements to the Kilns is this semicircular brick bench built into the hillside beside the pond.

ished for so long. In both cases, the stories they tell explore what is wrong with people. Tolkien and Lewis did not invent this feature of storytelling. It probably began with the very first story anyone sitting in a cave or huddled beside a campfire ever told. Storytelling explores the problem with people. Stories without conflict are bad stories that no one repeats. Conflict describes the reality of human life and interaction with others. The resolution of the conflict in which everyone lives happily ever after reflects the human yearning for hope.

The conflict and struggle in *The Hobbit* and *The Pilgrim's Regress* are not the kind that involve a contest with inanimate forces of nature, like the voyage of Columbus across the wild ocean or the expedition of Hillary to the summit of Mt. Everest. Tolkien's tale of adventure and treasure seeking is an old story like Homer's *Odyssey*. Lewis's allegory explores the war within John in which John is at conflict with himself. The travelers go from one adventure to the next. The episodes might easily be some other sort of adventures, but they all involve life-threatening encounters with other creatures that can think and reason. Bilbo and the dwarves are captured by murderous goblins (orcs) and hostile wood elves. They fall prey to bloodthirsty and flesh-hungry trolls and giant spiders. Bilbo matches wits with a sinister creature with a magic ring and an evil dragon with a horde of treasure. The symbolic equation of darkness with evil appears throughout *The Hobbit* as malice lurks in the deep caves under the mountains, in the

dense shadows of the forest, and under the cover of darkest night. Evil does not spring, however, from the mountains, the forests, or the night. Evil springs from the imaginations of those thinking creatures that choose the dark places as their dwelling.

In the final conflict of *The Hobbit*, Tolkien paints again the ancient picture of where greed, envy, malice, and pride always lead – thinking creatures set against one another in warfare. The poor hobbit laments his ignorance in not understanding war when he is the only one who recognizes its irrationality. Those that should be friends turn against one another until the moment when they are confronted by a greater external threat that forces them to cooperate in self-defense as they battle the corporate evil of the goblin army.

Above: The top of Shotover Hill still offers vistas toward the undeveloped land surrounding Oxford that was the rule before industry came to nearby Crowley.

Previous page: Jack Lewis spent time and energy clearing a path through the jungle of Shotover Hill that rises immediately in front of the Kilns.

Even as development crowds the base of Shotover Hill, the rural atmosphere that dominated when Jack and Warnie bought the Kilns can still be found.

The landscapes of Narnia and the Shire lay close at hand to the Inklings in the countryside around Oxford.

By 1937, the year Lewis wrote *Out of the Silent Planet* about a trip to Mars, the world political situation looked grim. Warnie had left China in 1932, as the Japanese were beginning their military campaign to conquer Asia. Hitler's rearmament and increasingly aggressive actions, beginning with the occupation of the Rhineland, had escalated until he annexed Austria and Czechoslovakia. Lewis later explained to Ruth Pitter that he took up science-fiction writing because he realized "what other planets in fiction are really good for: for *spiritual* adventures."[34] In *Out of the Silent Planet*, Lewis imagined a world in which the natives had no experience with treachery, deceit, theft, envy, pride, jealousy, vanity, greed, lust, prejudice, murder, or any of the other creative departures from normal human life that humans have conceived.

The greatest problem of communication between "earthlings" and the inhabitants of Mars is not simply one of language. In *Star Trek*, the 1960s television program about the voyages of the starship *Enterprise*, every planet the ship visited was inhabited by people who spoke English. Lewis solved the language problem by sending Dr. Elwin Ransom, a philologist like Tolkien, on the trip. The

Above: Creaking cranes now dominate the skyline of Oxford where the dreaming spires once reigned alone, but cows still graze in the expansive Port Meadow where the Inklings once walked on their way to the Perch at Binsey and the Trout at Wolvercote.

Following page: Cuckoo Lane allowed the Lewis brothers to bypass the congested shops of Headington and reach Oxford by way of Headington Hill Park.

Above: Jack and Warnie would have been greeted by Magdalen Tower as they crossed Magdalen Bridge when walking to town from Headington.

Previous page: Jack and Warnie may have taken the bus to and from Magdalen College, but they also enjoyed the walk along secluded Cuckoo Lane, a narrow foot path that parallels the busy road from Headington into Oxford.

greatest struggle for Ransom involved how to explain the flaws of human character to intelligent beings who had no frame of reference for understanding the self-destructive tendencies of human nature. He finally hit upon the idea of calling humans "bent." People from Earth do the things they do because they are "bent."

On the eve of World War II, Lewis uses the tale of an interplanetary space flight to explore the dark motives and aspirations of humans who have the capacity for great accomplishments, but who tend to turn their capacity toward what eventually causes the greatest harm to others. He explores the idea of the scientific imagination without any constraint, and how the search for knowledge can easily become bent into a quest for power. Ransom is kidnapped by Weston and Devine, a wealthy politician and a scientist who see themselves as the vanguard in the conquest of the solar system. To establish their beachhead on Mars, however, they believe the Martians expect them to turn over a human hostage as a sacrifice. When Ransom protests, one of his captors replies that he should not "be so small minded as to think that the rights or the life of an individual or of a million individuals are of the slightest importance in comparison with" their plans for the colonization of the universe.[35] In a

Narrow stone alleys provide convenient alternate routes through Oxford.
(Photo by Rebecca Whitten Poe)

letter to Arthur C. Clarke, Lewis laid out the problem: "I agree Technology is *per se* neutral: but a race devoted to the increase of its power by technology with complete indifference to ethics *does* seem to me a cancer in the universe. Certainly if he goes on his present course much further man can *not* be trusted with knowledge."[36]

What follows is an exploration of human misunderstanding based upon prejudice. Ransom escapes his captors only to find himself lost in a hostile landscape that he believes is filled with monsters. Creatures that do not take the human shape must be monsters. Ransom's "universe was peopled with horrors such as ancient and medieval mythology could hardly rival. No insect-like, vermiculate or crustacean Abominable, no twitching feelers, rasping wings, slimy coils, curling tentacles,

The Kilns and the surrounding countryside during the time Jack and Warnie lived there
(Used by permission of The Marion E. Wade Center, Wheaton College, Wheaton, IL.)

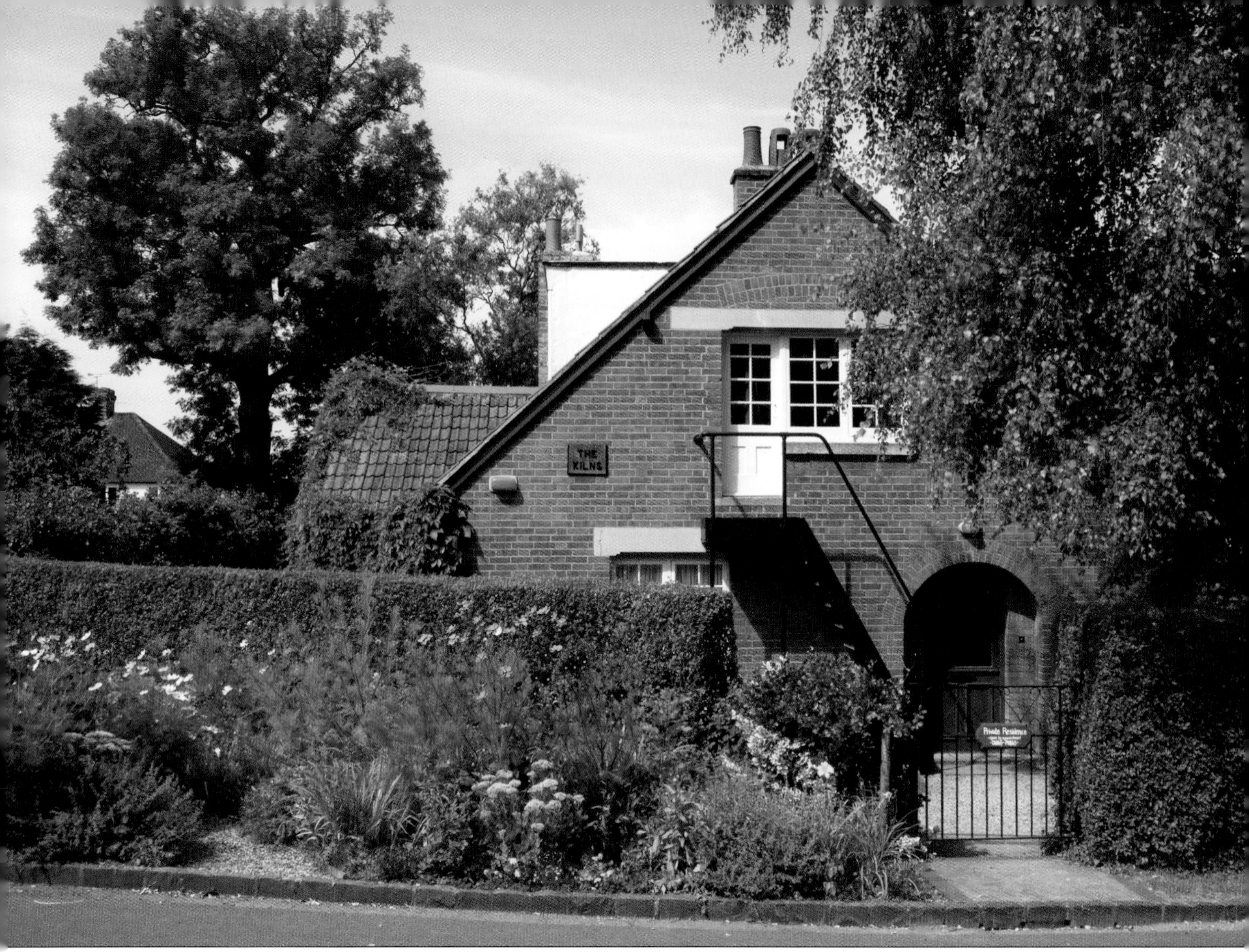

Above: The tradesmen's entrance to the Kilns showing the outside stairs Jack Lewis installed so that he could come and go to his bedroom without going through Janie Moore's bedroom

Previous page: When Jack and Warnie Lewis first bought the Kilns, the entire landscape looked much like this rare, remaining glimpse of pastoral England beside Holy Trinity Church.

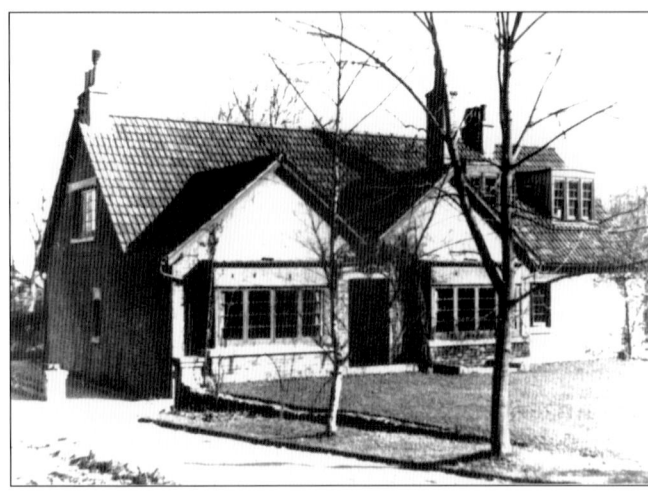

The Kilns as it looked when Jack and Warnie lived there

(Used by permission of The Marion E. Wade Center, Wheaton College, Wheaton, IL.)

no monstrous union of superhuman intelligence and insatiable cruelty seemed to him anything but likely on an alien world."[37] He meets three different species of intelligent life, but none of them are monsters, nor do they have enmity against one another. He expects that one must be the "master race" and the others the servants, because that is the way things are done on Earth. This kind of reasoning, however, proves to be "bent" thinking. Lewis illustrates that the highest achievement of civilization, which is rational thought, is susceptible to the same corruption as our most base passions.

While Ransom assumes that inhabitants of Mars will be monsters who will do terrible things to him, Weston and Devine regard the Martians as subhuman "savages." Devine believes the only way to deal with "natives" is to intimidate them with threats. Weston, on the other hand, believes he knows the rules for frightening and then conciliating primitive races. He offers them colored beads from Woolworth's department store. Lewis exposes the foolish conceit by which people judge others who are different as Weston and Devine condescend and patronize the Martians while trying to dominate them. It worked for Hitler in his negotiations with the French and British. Weston and Devine represent the bent human race to the universe, and even Ransom must recognize the degree to which he also bears the traits of being bent.

THE JOURNEY

What the fantasy, science fiction, and allegory that Tolkien and Lewis wrote all had in common was that their characters all went on journeys. Journey formed the central organizing principle for Tolkien's tales of hobbits, but journey also formed the central plotline for all of Lewis's fictional books except *The Screwtape Letters.*

Seventy years later *The Allegory of Love*, Lewis's great study of the medieval allegorical love-poetry tradition, continues to be the standard from which all contemporary scholars must depart in their agreement or disagreement. (Lewis would take up the theme of love many more times, most notably in *The Four Loves.*) In a world that has lost its poetry, Lewis explained how allegory works. While symbolism deals with the external world to which people relate, allegory refers to the internal world of thoughts and feelings. The best allegory deals with the internal struggles of intellect and feelings mediated by character (Lewis would expound on this idea in *The Abolition of Man*). Lewis argued that this warfare within, or the *bellum intestinum* (in this first scholarly work, Lewis expects the reader to know Latin!), is best expressed by a journey rather than a war. John Bunyan, the last great allegorist who closes the fifteen-hundred-year tradition with *The Pilgrim's Progress* (1678), demonstrates how the spiritual life can be represented as a journey from the City of Destruction to the Heavenly City. Bunyan also wrote *The Holy War* (1682) in which he describes the process of salvation as a war between Shaddai and Diabolis for the town of Mansoul, but the war imagery has not had the staying power of the journey. Lewis remarked "that only the crudest allegory will represent [the *bellum intestinum*] by a pitched battle" which is why "the *Pilgrim's Progress* is a better book than the *Holy War.*"[38]

The Tolkiens and the Havards attended St. Aloysius Catholic Church just beyond the Eagle and Child on the Woodstock Road.

The hammer beam ceiling in the great hall at Christ Church College is one of the finest in England.

Above: Tourists flock to see the great hall at Christ Church College since it was used as the model for the hall of Hogwarts' School in the Harry Potter series.

Following page: Jack Lewis liked nothing better than to charge across the countryside on the walking paths that crisscross the English landscape.

The lions that ornament the ceiling at Christ Church College, and litter the Oxford landscape generally, may have provided the inspiration for Aslan.

While Lewis worked for years on his scholarly study of allegory, he dashed off *The Pilgrim's Regress* during a fortnight while vacationing with Arthur Greeves in Belfast in 1932. It describes his spiritual experience leading to his conversion and what lies beyond. Just as Bunyan (in *The Pilgrim's Progress*) describes spiritual experiences as places and characters, such as the Slough of Despond, Vanity Fair, Doubting Castle, and Giant Despair, Lewis describes all of the emotional and intellectual fancies into which he was drawn before his conversion. His conversion, however, does not mean escape from the world. Instead, it means that he must now return and deal with all of these old charms as a Christian. At the opening of *The Allegory of Love*, Lewis acknowledged that most people today cannot understand allegory; therefore, he did not write *The Pilgrim's Regress* for a large, popular audience.

While Lewis read to the Inklings from his scholarly work in progress and his completed allegorical biography, Tolkien read to them about hobbits. The subtitle of this first hobbit tale reflects what Tolkien also grasped about the significance of the journey. He named his book *The Hobbit: or There and Back Again* (1937). The hobbit Bilbo Baggins is not the same person at the end of his journey that he was when he began. The spiritual journey changes people into something else. Some refuse to go on the journey. Some who go on the journey refuse to be changed by the journey. Lewis and Tolkien both grasped the artistic beauty of the simple understanding that life is a journey. Just as Tolkien and Dyson helped Lewis grasp why the death and resurrection of Jesus fulfills the longing after the dying and rising god mythology found in every culture, they understood that every culture prizes the story of the journey. The Bible contains stories from many cultures over many centuries in which the journey figures prominently. Abram left

Ur of the Chaldees and became Abraham. The slaves of Egypt journeyed to the Promised Land and became the nation of Israel. Jesus journeyed from Galilee to Jerusalem to die. More eloquently, the writer of Hebrews says of the journey of the Son of God from heaven to earth and back again, "who for the joy set before him endured the cross, scorning its shame, and sat down at the right hand of the throne of God" (Hebrews 12:2).

Jack wrote *Out of the Silent Planet* during 1937. As mentioned before, the journey results in new self-awareness and a change so that the hero will never be the same again. This book had actually come as the result of a dare between Lewis and Tolkien, who agreed that Lewis would write a space-travel story and Tolkien would write a time-travel story. Tolkien's story was "The Lost Road," which his publisher Allen and Unwin declined to publish. Lewis's tale was also turned down by J. M. Dent and Sons before the Bodley Head finally agreed to publish it.

So often we hear that writers should write about what they know if they expect to write successfully. What exactly did Tolkien know about hobbits and Lewis about space travel? As it turns out, quite a lot. Tolkien once said that Sam Gamgee was a "reflexion of the English soldier" he had known during the Great War.[39] Tolkien's hobbits are bachelors who like to eat, drink, and smoke weed. Bilbo and his close relative Frodo live in a most comfortable house set in its own grounds at the base of the Hill. Jack and Warnie lived most comfortably in the Kilns at the foot of Shotover Hill, a landmark in Oxfordshire for centuries, which is even designated on John Speed's map of 1611. In fact, the tradesmen's entrance of the Kilns is exactly as Tolkien describes the entry and arrangement of rooms at Bag-End, with all the best rooms on the left and windows facing the garden. When restoration of the Kilns began after many years of decline, the ceilings appeared to be painted a yellowish shade when one would normally expect to find white. On closer inspection, however, the ceilings were actually stained with forty years

Above: Warnie Lewis kept his cabin cruiser, the *Bosphorus*, docked at Salters boat yard at Folly Bridge.

Opposite page: While Jack Lewis walked at breakneck speed, Tolkien loved to take his time and notice the flowers, the twigs, and the twists of the branches overhead.

Warnie Lewis enjoyed the river life in the same vicinity as Ratty and Mole in Kenneth Graham's *Wind in the Willows*.

Henry II kept his mistress, the fair Rosalind, at Godstow Abbey on the river near the Trout. Henry's wife Eleanor of Aquitaine insisted she had nothing to do with poor Rosalind's unfortunate death. These stones provided a connection between Lewis and the courtly love tradition he loved.

of nicotine from the brothers' two-pack-a-day habit! The brothers also saw no special necessity for ash trays since they reasoned that cigarette ash would keep the moths away. They merely ground their ashes into the carpets!

To claim that Jack and Warnie were Bilbo and Frodo pushes matters too far and does not take into account how imagination works. Tolkien "created" Bilbo and Frodo, but people do not create out of nothing as God does. Human creativity expands upon what we find in the world. At one point Bilbo has qualities we might find in Warnie. After all, Warnie had been to China, just as Bilbo went off on a great adventure. At another point, however, Warnie may have contributed to Samwise, who was such a faithful companion to Frodo. On the other hand, the Lewis brothers also had a gardener named Paxford who bears certain resemblances to Tolkien's description of Gaffer Gamgee, the father of Sam.

At the end of the Lord of the Rings, when the ring has been destroyed, Aragorn has been crowned king, and everyone should live happily ever after, the hobbits return to Hobbiton. They find it in a state of desolation: avenues of trees have been cut down, gardens are neglected, rows of ugly houses have replaced beautiful spaces, and a tall chimney pours black smoke from a mill. Something similar happened to the Lewis brothers and their beautiful estate at the foot of Shotover Hill. In 1935, Jack Lewis complained in a letter to Arthur Greeves that his home was being ruined by the construction of "council houses" along Kiln Lane, which had occurred as a result of the expansion of the Morris Motors factory about a mile from the Kilns.[40] The open English countryside to which the Lewis brothers had moved in 1930 had become an industrial town.

As for the "fellowship of the ring," Tolkien needed to look no further than the motley crew that gathered in Lewis's rooms every Thursday night. They were as diverse as hobbits, dwarves, and elves. Tolkien, who grew up as an impoverished Catholic raised by a single mother after the early death of his father, would have known something of prejudice in the Protestant England of the Edwardian age in which he grew up. Another member of the Inklings, Lord David Cecil, on the other hand, belonged to one of the most prominent families in the kingdom. The younger son of the fourth Marquess of Salisbury, Cecil grew up at Hatfield House, the ancestral estate given by Elizabeth I to Sir Robert Cecil, her Lord Chancellor. Since that time, the Cecil family has supplied a total of four heads of government to their sovereign. Jack and Warnie were products of a thoroughly middle class home, the sons of a police-court solicitor, while Nevill Coghill's father was a baronet. Coghill and the Lewis brothers all came from the Ireland that existed before the Easter Uprising of 1917, while Colin Hardie came from Scotland. The Inklings embodied a thousand years of prejudice, malice, enmity, class conflict, ethnic warfare, and strife. Like the fellowship of the ring in Tolkien's epic novel, a stronger power than these evils prevailed among the Inklings, who came to personify friendship, about which Lewis would write a great deal in *The Four Loves*.

Lewis also relied upon the familiar in his tale of interplanetary travel, for the story begins with a man walking vigorously across an English countryside following a thunderstorm, who realizes that he must push further on if he expects to find an inn that night. Whenever Jack Lewis had spare time or a holiday, he spent it charging across the countryside of England, Ireland, Wales, or Scotland. His letters and Warnie's diaries overflow with descriptions of their walking tours. Lewis's hero "wasted no time on the landscape" but surged ahead, exactly like the Lewis brothers, who enjoyed the walk but spent it talking rather than looking. Tolkien, on the other hand, enjoyed the walk in order to see the landscape, frequently dawdling behind on their excursions together. The hero of Lewis's first science-fiction story is a philologist, like Tolkien. So we see Lewis borrowing here and there from his own familiar world to create the world of his imagination in *Out of the Silent Planet*.

Jack, Hugo, and Humphrey stopped at the Trout for supper on the first night of their boating trip in August 1939. They frequently made the journey in the years ahead by foot or motor car.

The Inklings seemed to be involved in some sort of perpetual journey for people who had a settled lifestyle. Hugo Dyson's very participation in the Inklings required his regular journeys from the University of Reading some twenty-five miles to the south of Oxford. Warnie made the longest journey to join the Inklings when he returned from China at the end of 1932. Immediately following his return and retirement from the army, he and Jack set off on what would prove to be their second annual walking tour in January 1933. Jack had induced Warnie to take one of these robust excursions with him in January 1931 when they set off on New Year's Day and walked for fifty-four miles from Chepstow. By January 1934, Warnie described the January walking tour as an "annual walk" that again took them along the river Wye. The third walk brought with it the kind of weather one might have expected in January as Jack and Warnie walked for hours across open country in the rain. Warnie wrote in his diary that "with the exception of some experiences during the war, I don't remember ever having had a more damnable walk. . . ." Warnie thought of swearing off these walking tours with Jack, but glorious vistas of still unspoiled countryside drew him back the next year. In January 1935 the walking tour kept them closer to home in the Chilten Hills near Oxford. For the 1936 walking tour, the brothers ventured north into Derbyshire. The 1937 tour took them to Dulverton in Somerset, while the 1938 excursion involved

The Trout continues to be a favorite spot for evening dining beside the river.

over fifty miles of walking through Wiltshire. The last of these annual walking tours came in January 1939 with a forty-two-mile stroll through the Welsh Marshes, after which the combination of war, age, and the vicissitudes of life foreclosed the holiday walks in the bleak midwinter.[41]

Warnie came to the walking trips late, for Jack had other walking partners who took part in his strenuous journeys. Jack went on an annual walking tour with Owen Barfield every spring from 1927 until the outbreak of World War II. A variety of friends joined these walks at different times, including W. O. Fields and Cecil Harwood, who were friends from Lewis's undergraduate days; Dom Bede Griffiths, who had been one of Lewis's students; and Tolkien.[42] These walks took the friends through the Berkshire and Wiltshire downs, the Salisbury Plain, the Cotswolds, Exmoor, Dorset, the Chilterns, and the Quantocks in the West Country.[43]

C. S. Lewis and other Inklings in front of the Trout
(Used by permission of The Marion E. Wade Center, Wheaton College, Wheaton, IL.)

In 1936, Warnie bought a twenty-foot cabin cruiser with two sleeping berths that he named the *Bosphorus*. In the Boxen tales that Jack and Warnie wrote during their childhood, the *Bosphorus* is the name of a ship in a story written by Jack.[44] He kept his boat at Salter's Boatyard at Folly Bridge in Oxford, where the Abingdon Road crosses the Isis.[45] The boat was perfect for cruising the inland canals and rivers of the midlands, for she only drew one foot ten inches of water. Warnie planned to take Jack and Hugo Dyson on one of his "ditch crawling" trips in August 1939.

Before the trip commenced, however, the international crisis worsened. Warnie was notified of his impending recall to active duty, which came with a promotion to major. While Warnie struggled in limbo until ordered to report for duty at Catterick, Yorkshire, Jack and Hugo decided to continue with their cruise. They enlisted R. E. Havard to skipper the boat for them. Havard, a local physician and member of the Inklings, had received the nickname "Humphrey" from Dyson.

The party left Folly Bridge on Saturday, August 26, and sailed up the Isis beyond the precincts of Oxford where it once again became the Thames. They crept from pub to pub, sampling all the beer they could, until they reached the Trout at Godstow, where they stopped for supper. They made their way up the river from there through the darkness to Newbridge, where Lewis and Dyson stayed in a room at the Rose Revived while Havard slept on the *Bosphorus*. On Sunday morning they cruised as far as Tadpole Bridge, where they tied up while they walked to the village of Buckland to attend services – Havard to the Catholic church and Lewis and Dyson to the Anglican. Over the next week they stopped at Radcot, Lechlade, and Inglesham, some thirty miles upstream from Oxford. Along the way back home, the engine broke down, which forced Lewis and Dyson to tow the boat downstream by rope while walking along the footpath until the engine was returned to service. By Friday they were back at the Trout, where they learned that Germany had invaded Poland. War was on.[46]

CHAPTER

THREE

War and Its Aftermath

When war came, Jack Lewis thought he might be called up again just as his brother had been. Of course, Warnie had been regular army. Jack also wondered if Oxford would close. After all, in the First World War entire colleges were emptied of men and taken over by the army and government. When he heard that the New Building in Magdalen in which his rooms were located would be taken over by the government, he packed up all his books and carried them to the basement. With mixed relief he carried them all back upstairs when he learned he had done all that work for naught and that Oxford would not close its doors for Hitler. Jack and the other Inklings would have different work to do during the war. The most important thing they did was to continue doing what they had always done.

With undergraduates and dons concerned about the disruption of their lives, Canon T. R. Milford asked Jack to preach at evensong on October 22, 1939, in the University Church of St. Mary the Virgin. The sermon is now printed as "Learning in War-Time," but Milford distributed mimeographed copies with the title "None Other Gods: Culture in War-Time." In the face of a conflict in which heaven and hell stood in the balance, Lewis acknowledged that some

The pulpit of St. Mary the Virgin Church where Lewis preached on several occasions during the war

Opposite page: St. Mary the Virgin, the University Church, stands between the High Street and the Radcliffe Camera. Here Lewis preached "Learning in War-Time" and "The Weight of Glory" in the early days of the war.

The Inklings continued to meet each Thursday night during the war in Lewis's rooms (identified by the two windows above the wisteria) at Magdalen College.

The Spaldings' house on South Park where Charles Williams stayed during the war disappeared some years ago to make way for the Zoology and Psychology building at the far end of the street on the right.

might wonder how anyone could spend any of their brief time on earth "on such comparative trivialities as literature or art, mathematics or biology."[47] Lewis rejected any thought of pitting the everyday duties and pleasures of life against what some might regard the "religious life." Lewis insisted that culture matters and that if Christians suspended their intellectual and aesthetic activity, they "would only succeed in substituting a worse cultural life for a better."[48] In short, Lewis explained that Christians have a duty to develop and use whatever gifts they may have without worrying about what the future might bring.

Jack offered to train cadets for the officer corps, but when his offer was declined, he joined the Oxford City Home Guard, who would be England's last line of defense in case of an invasion. His duty began every Saturday at 1:30 in the morning and lasted until early dawn during which time he plodded through the darkened streets of Oxford searching for signs of German paratroopers. He celebrated his first night of duty with a small dinner with Hugo Dyson and Humphrey Havard followed by an extraordinary Friday evening meeting of the Inklings.

War also affected the Tolkien household. The eldest son, John, who was studying for the priesthood in Rome, was evacuated to Lancashire when hostilities broke out between the United Kingdom and Italy. The second son, Michael, became an antiaircraft gunner after leaving Trinity College. The third son, Christopher, only turned fifteen the year of the war and was too young to serve, but he went up to Oxford as a member of Trinity College. In 1944, Christopher was called up to serve in the RAF. The departure of the boys left only Priscilla, the youngest, at home with her parents as the war began. Like Lewis, Tolkien took on war duties as an air-raid warden.

Because of overcrowding, Charles Williams never had an office in the Oxford offices of the Oxford University Press.

Of the other Inklings, Dr. Humphrey Havard was called up in 1943 to serve as a medical officer in the navy. He grew a beard while in service, which came out red and earned him the new nickname of the Red Admiral, which was added to the nickname given by Warnie: Useless Quack. In due course, however, Havard was transferred to duty in Oxford with a malaria research unit through a connection of Tolkien's. Tolkien said it was his only successful case of pulling strings, but Lewis dubbed him "The Lord of the Strings."[49] Once the "phony war" was over and Hitler invaded the Lowlands in spring 1940, the war began in earnest for Warnie, who was stationed in France. He was evacuated from Dunkirk with the bulk of the British Expeditionary Force in one of the most gallant maneuvers in military history, as Englishmen in small boats ferried the troops to safety. By August, Warnie was transferred to reserve duty and returned to Oxford, where he served with the Oxford City Home Guards, spending much of his time on the *Bosphorus*, which he painted battleship grey, as part of the Upper Thames Patrol.[50] Though Havard and Warnie returned to Oxford, Adam Fox left for good in 1942 when he accepted a post as Canon of Westminster Abbey.

Charles Williams writing
(Used by permission of The Marion E. Wade Center, Wheaton College, Wheaton, IL.)

Wadham College where Lord David Cecil served as fellow in the 1920s

The tower of New College rises beyond the Bridge of Sighs. Lord David Cecil became a fellow of New College in 1939.

The Inklings changed as a result of the war. Friends departed, but new friends joined the little group. Charles Williams, who had visited the Inklings on several occasions during the 1930s, quickly became a central figure. When war broke out, Oxford University Press evacuated its staff from London and moved back to Oxford. Charles Williams, who had worked at the Press since 1908, moved up to Oxford in September 1939. Williams found rooms with the Spalding family on South Parks Road. Ruth Spalding, one of the daughters, had met Williams when she produced his play *Seed of Adam* at the University Church. Williams' wife, Michal, stayed in London with their seventeen-year-old son, Michael, preferring the Blitz to life in Oxford. Theirs was not a happy marriage, and the domestic complications of multiple generations of Spaldings living together in one house did not seem conducive to anyone's tranquility. Williams would live in Oxford during the week, but returned to his family in London for the weekends throughout the war.

Lord David Cecil held a post at Wadham College as Fellow and Lecturer in Modern History from 1924 until 1930, but he left to devote himself to writing. He had published his first book, *The Stricken Deer*, which was a biography of the poet and hymn writer William Cowper, in 1929. In the course of the 1930s he wrote books about Sir Walter Scott, Jane Austen, Lord Melville, and the Victorian novelists. In 1939, however, he returned to Oxford as a Fellow in English Literature at New College. He and his wife kept a flat in Saville House, one of New College's properties on Mansfield Road.

Not all the Inklings had the same literary background or preparation as Lewis, Tolkien, Coghill, and Dyson. Humphrey Havard and Warnie Lewis were not the only exceptions. During the war, Commander Jim Dundas-

The great hall of New College

Grant came to Oxford to command the Oxford University Naval Division. He stayed at Magdalen College where he met Lewis, and the two became fast friends. Lewis then introduced him to the Inklings, and he became a regular attender.

The Inklings did not always agree about their primary purpose in gathering. Tolkien and Lewis believed that someone always needed to read something they were writing at the time. Havard usually reminded everyone that he was not a literary man. Dyson, a literary man, wrote very little in his long career, but he loved to talk with people who loved to talk and who had

Above: The cloisters of New College
Following page: New College chapel viewed from the cloisters

A series of carved angels ornament the beamed roof of New College chapel.

New College chapel

interesting things to say. As a result, Dyson did not care for the readings. For his part, Warnie hated the philosophical discussions that inevitably developed. Warnie noted in his diary, "I finished lunch today feeling that if I were Emperor of the World, I would start a pogrom against philosophers."[51]

THE INFLUENCE OF CHARLES WILLIAMS

In coming to Oxford, Charles Williams brought with him a different world of experience from the cosmopolitan city of London, where he had lived and worked for so many years. Likewise, Lord David Cecil had traveled in different kinds of circles all his life. Both of them shared an appreciation for someone whom Jack Lewis deplored: T. S. Eliot. Lewis blamed Eliot for destroying poetry with the publication of "The Wasteland." Traditional forms of poetry that had prevailed since time immemorial came crashing down. Eliot changed the fashion of poetry at a time when Lewis had the ambition to become a great poet. "The Wasteland" dashed Lewis's hopes, and poetry receded into the background as Lewis realized he could not compete in the strange new world of modern poetry. Eliot, however, was a great admirer of the novels of Charles Williams. Lady Ottoline Morrell, the great literary hostess of London, invited both men to one of her famous teas for the purpose of their introduction. Lord David Cecil belonged to this same set. They would never become close friends, but their mutual respect only grew as Eliot became the editor of Williams' books published by Faber and Faber, where Eliot worked. Williams could not be enthusiastic about Eliot's poetry because of its lack of objective meaning that could be understood by a reader, but he appreciated Eliot nonetheless. Eliot and Williams had other points of disagreement, notably their views on Milton.

When Charles Williams came to Oxford, Milton's *Paradise Lost* had been out of favor for years. No one on the English faculty lectured on it. At the same time, Lewis wanted to do something for Williams to make him more a part of the university. Though Williams had not completed a degree in his formal education, Lewis managed to smuggle him onto the lecture list due to the shortage of teachers during the war. Williams chose to lecture on Milton and refute more than a century of prejudice and ignorance about *Paradise Lost*. Lewis pronounced the lectures a roaring success, so much so that Lewis decided that he would take on Milton himself. The result of this resolution came in the form of the Ballard Matthews Lectures delivered at University College in North Wales in 1941 on *Paradise Lost*, which Lewis published in 1942 as *A Preface to Paradise Lost*.

If Williams influenced Lewis to pursue scholarly work on *Paradise Lost*, that influence began to multiply as Lewis's imagination interacted with his research. In *A Preface to Paradise Lost*, Lewis made the observation that Satan hates to be ridiculed or laughed at and that Milton knew that Satan really was "an ass." During a particularly boring sermon one Sunday morning at Holy Trinity Church in Headington, while Warnie was still on active duty, Lewis began turning over in his mind the idea for a story about a senior devil who gives advice to a junior devil on his first assignment.[52] The fruit of this little idea was published in a series of articles in a religious journal named *The Guardian* and published as a book in 1942 under the title *The Screwtape Letters*. With that little bit of imaginative overflow from his scholarly work, C. S. Lewis was propelled from relative academic obscurity into public notice and fame.

Lewis had attempted to write a sequel to his science fiction novel about space travel, but it had not gone anywhere. That first attempt was published posthumously as the fragment *The Dark Tower*. Reflection on Milton's retelling of the temptation of Adam and Eve, however, led Lewis to write a new sequel to *Out of the Silent Planet* in which he imagined what it might be like if Satan had failed in his temptation. He set this new tale on Venus and called it *Perelandra*. It was published in 1943.

Williams also had a great interest in the King Arthur legends. In 1938 he had published a cycle of poems, which he called *Taliessin through Logres*, based on the Arthurian tales. All the while he lived

The Hall of New College dates from the fourteenth century and seats 200 at meals.

Lord David Cecil lived at Savile House, one of the New College properties on Mansfield Road, during the war.

Above: The ghastly gargoyles and tormented carved figures that ornament the medieval buildings of Oxford remind us that Screwtape and his fellows are a busy lot. (Photo by Ben Dockery)

Previous page: The great oak tree in the cloister quad of New College where Professor Moody turned Draco Malfoy into a ferret in *Harry Potter and the Goblet of Fire*

Jack's and Warnie's short pew against the north wall of Holy Trinity Church has been commemorated by a small brass plaque.

in Oxford, he worked on a second volume from which he read regularly to the Inklings. Williams had also written part of a piece entitled "The Figure of Arthur" as well as a piece of criticism entitled "Commentary on the Arthurian Poems." Discussions of Arthur, Merlin, and the days when Christianity first came to Britain's shores animated the Inklings' discussions during the war. Williams' influence appears in the last of Lewis's science fiction novels, *That Hideous Strength*, which incorporates Merlin full blown in the twentieth century while also using Williams' term Logres, a pre-Roman name for Britain.

Above: Lewis's "war work" included lectures to the men at the RAF fields that may still be seen near Oxford.

Previous page: During a Sunday service at Holy Trinity Church in Headington, Jack Lewis had the idea for Screwtape.

WAR WORK

During the war, people did things they would never have done on their own. The war effort meant that people "did their bit." Jack Lewis never planned to write popular books of theology and apologetics for nonacademic readers. The war changed all that. In the fall of 1939 and into the winter of 1940, Jack wrote *The Problem of Pain* at the invitation of Ashley Sampson, editor of a popular theology series of books called the Christian Challenge Series. Sampson had read *The Pilgrim's Regress* and thought Lewis was just the person to write a book on the problem of suffering, perhaps the greatest intellectual and existential challenge to Christianity. Lewis was a good choice, but to have made the choice on the basis of *The Pilgrim's Regress* seems quite bizarre since it is perhaps Lewis's most inaccessible book.

The chapel at Somerville College provided a center of worship where Stella Aldwinckle cared for the spiritual needs of the female students while hatching the Socratic Club.

Lewis often lectured to hundreds in the East Lecture Hall on the upper floor of the Examinations School Building while Tolkien lectured in the small rooms on the ground floor that accommodated twenty or thirty. Lord David Cecil was the other great lecturer in Oxford in those days.

The Problem of Pain went into three printings in 1940 and continued into more printings from that time to the present day. Lewis appeared to have a knack for explaining difficult ideas to the common person.

On the basis of the success of *The Problem of Pain*, James Welch asked Lewis to prepare four fifteen-minute talks to be given over the BBC in August 1941 as part of their religious broadcasting schedule. Lewis decided to talk about the natural law, because so many people in Britain had lost an understanding of right and wrong. People may say that everything is relative, but they change their mind when they become the object of injustice. We know something is wrong when it happens to us much more easily than when we do it to someone else. Lewis also drew the distinction between local cultural rules, related to local preferences, and the universal standards that people in cultures all over the world have acknowledged across time. People may have different preferences for what constitutes beauty, but they understand the common concept of beauty. From the existence of this universal understanding of "decent behavior" or the natural law, Lewis moves to the source of the idea: the Law Giver. He named this series of talks "Right and Wrong: A Clue to the Meaning of the Universe."

The BBC had such a good response to Lewis's four talks that they invited him back for a second series in which he moved to the next logical step. He discussed "What Christians Believe." He did not expound Protestant or Catholic doctrine. He did not discuss mode of baptism or church government. He did not discuss how to calculate the return of Christ through the prophecies of Ezekiel and Daniel cross-referenced with Revelation. He spoke about what all Christians believe. He focused on the common faith that unites Christians. He gave reasons for why Christians believe what they believe about God entering into the world in physical form as Jesus of Nazareth. He explained why it makes good sense. Again, the public responded positively. Lewis published the two series of talks as *Broadcast Talks* in July 1942.

Opposite page: When the war began, Jack built a concrete bomb shelter beside the pond at the foot of Shotover Hill.

Above: The bomb shelter was well built but small.

In fall 1942, Lewis broadcast his third series with the BBC. This time Lewis took as his subject "Christian Behaviour." Instead of focusing on the stereotypical expectations of the public about Christian legalism, Lewis did not stress sin and vice. Instead he discussed the Christian virtues of faith, hope, charity, and forgiveness. He stressed that life in Christ, the living Lord, is a positive experience rather than a negative effort at self-improvement. This series was published separately as *Christian Behaviour* in 1943.

Lewis presented his fourth and final BBC series of seven talks beginning in fall 1943 and going into winter 1944. He named this series "Beyond Personality: The Christian View of God." This series moved more profoundly into the mystery of the relationship between a believer and Christ. He discussed how Christ actually affects a person and changes them. He made clear that Christianity is not merely the gift wrapping that people may see in religious practices, but that the practices reflect a union that has taken place with God through the work of Christ Jesus. This last series was published as *Beyond Personality* in 1944. The public and the BBC asked for more talks, but Jack declined. When he had

The Inklings had continued to meet at the Eagle and Child on Tuesday mornings during the war, except when too many servicemen or the beer shortage forced them to other quarters.

When beer ran out at the Eagle and Child during the war, the Inklings retreated to the White Horse next to Blackwell's Bookshop.

The King's Arms near Blackwell's Bookshop was another pub where the Inklings found beer during the war.

begun his talks, Britain stood alone against Hitler. By the end of his fourth talk, the Normandy invasion had changed everything and the outcome of the war seemed assured. In 1952 Lewis published the four series in a single volume he called *Mere Christianity*. The broadcasts and the publication of them on both sides of the Atlantic had produced a flood of letters with all manner of questions that Jack felt obliged to answer. Warnie typed all of his correspondence but had no time for his own interests.

Lewis's war work also included giving talks at RAF stations around the country in 1941. Warnie was his tour manager. He lectured at nearby stations during terms and throughout the country during the long summer vacation. In January 1942 he took up a new duty through the insistence of Miss Stella Aldwinckle, a formidable lady who served as a chaplain at Somerville College. Miss Aldwinckle recognized the need for some public forum where intellectual issues related to religion could be discussed openly, and she designated Lewis as president of the proposed university organization that she named the Socratic Club. Lewis saw the value of the club, and as one who had long championed such clubs, he agreed to help. A paper on some intellectual issue was read at each meeting with an opposing response by a Christian or unbeliever. Lewis added star attraction and Stella Aldwinckle added tenacious attention to planning and execution. The meetings hosted some of the greatest Christian and atheist minds of the age. Jack's enthusiasm for the Socratic Club proved greater than the war, for he continued his weekly involvement throughout his remaining time at Oxford.

DOING GOOD WORK

The war prevented Lewis from working on any major scholarly projects, though he finally began work in 1944 on a volume in the Oxford History of English Literature series that Oxford University Press had commissioned in 1935. Instead, he wrote little books on a variety of subjects. The adult books for which he is most famous come from this period. The other Inklings were equally busy. Because of his scholarly publications in the 1920s and 1930s, Tolkien had a solid reputation and could afford a few years of "silence" in the scholarly press. In fact, he had not written anything for his scholarly colleagues since 1937. He was consumed with the struggle for Middle Earth and the efforts of one small hobbit and his friends to destroy the ring of power. Tolkien labored away to get the story right for years. He had nothing else to read to the Inklings unless he wrote down a bit of light verse, but the Inklings urged him on, except for Hugo Dyson, who merely collapsed back on Jack's sofa and moaned, "Oh, not more elves."

Charles Williams churned out the work. During the war he published *Witchcraft* (1941), *The Forgiveness of Sins* (1942), *The Figure of Beatrice* (1943), *The Region of Summer Stars* (1944), *All Hallows' Eve* (1945), and *The House of the Octopus* (1945).

Lord David Cecil managed to be as productive as a fully employed fellow as he had been as an independent writer. During the war he published *The English Poets* (1941), *Oxford Book of Christian Verse* (1941), *Men of the RAF* (1942), *Hardy the Novelist: An Essay in Criticism* (1942), *Anthony and Cleopatra* (1944), and *Poetry of Thomas Grey* (1945). The last three of these were originally prepared for named lectureships: the Clark Lectures, the W. P. Ker Memorial Lecture, and the Warton Lecture. Cecil was extremely popular as a lecturer in Oxford, a rarified class that probably only included Lewis. He was sought after for company because of his good disposition as much as for his interesting, enthusiastic, and clever way of saying things that combined with a grand breadth of

Once a rarity, female students now share the university with men.
(Photo by Rebecca Whitten Poe)

Dorothy L. Sayers' friendship with Lewis, Williams, and other Inklings gave her another connection to the city of her birth. A blue plaque identifies the house at 1 Brewer Street across from Christ Church College where she was born.

knowledge. Surprisingly, he had a most unexpected trait. According to Warnie Lewis, he was "perhaps the worst reader of his own works in Oxford."[53] The one worse, of course, was Tolkien. After the war, his son Christopher joined the Inklings and took over the task of reading the new installments of "The New Hobbit," as they referred to the yet unnamed Lord of the Rings.

No one expected Warnie Lewis to contribute anything to an Inklings meeting except his good company, thoughtful opinion, and well-brewed tea. From the time Warnie returned from China, he had devoted himself to collecting the Lewis family papers into massive scrapbooks. With this work completed and his military service behind him, Warnie began a new project for his own pleasure that came as a surprise to everyone. In 1942 he began writing what would become *The Splendid Century*, a history of the reign of Louis XIV of France. He had actually begun the project as early as 1934, but he came back to it in earnest during the war.[54] In a letter to his son Christopher in 1944, Tolkien remarked that Warnie was "writing a book: it's catching."[55] From then on, Warnie read regularly from the books he began writing about France during the reign of the Sun King.

Hugo Dyson wrote very little, so he did not look to the Inklings for the kind of encouragement and criticism that the others enjoyed. On one occasion in the Eagle and Child, a question arose as to whether Tolkien's speech or Dyson's handwriting created the greatest difficulty for their friends. Jack remarked, "Well, there's this to be said for Hugo's writing, there's less of it."[56]

LIVING IN WARTIME

As air-raid wardens, Lewis and Tolkien understood what it would mean if the Nazis decided to bomb Oxford. It would have made sense from a military perspective because of the research being conducted there and at Cambridge into the potential of atomic energy as a weapon of war. Air-raid wardens had the responsibility of insuring that no light could be seen from any house at night. Every window had to be heavily draped. At the Kilns, old army blankets hung on every window. Twelve years after the war ended, Jack Lewis's new bride found the army blankets still hanging in the windows!

While the blankets prevented the Nazis from having a clear target, they did not protect from exploding bombs. For protection, Jack Lewis

Dorothy L. Sayers spent her undergraduate days at Somerville College on the Woodstock Road just north of the Eagle and Child.

At Somerville College, Dorothy L. Sayers found a community that could nurture her young intellect until she blossomed into one of the great Christian apologists of the twentieth century.

instructed Paxford, the gardener, to dig a bomb shelter in the garden. He chose a spot beside the pond where he could dig into the side of Shotover Hill. Rather than the kind of makeshift bomb shelter that often appeared in English gardens, the bomb shelter at the Kilns was more than a damp hole in the ground. It was a massive work of poured concrete covered by tons of earth.

When the bombing of London began, tens of thousands of children were evacuated to the countryside and to Canada. Many children would be separated from their parents for the duration of the war. In some cases, children simply lived with other families as part of the family. Children were taken in to handle household chores like cleaning, washing clothes, and ironing. In other cases, children worked in shops or on farms to help the families that gave them shelter. A number of children lived at the Kilns during the war. A young girl named Jill Flewett, whom Warnie and Jack soon nicknamed June, came to live at the Kilns in 1943 and remained until she went to drama school in London in 1945. Jack and Warnie would remain deeply devoted to her until they died. In his diary the day before she left for school, Warnie wrote that the seventeen-year-old girl was one of those rare people for whom the word "saintly" applies.[57] She took the stage name Jill Raymond and made her film debut in 1947 with Jean Simmons in *Woman in the Hall*.

Dorothy L. Sayers
(Used by permission of The Marion E. Wade Center, Wheaton College, Wheaton, IL.)

The war produced shortages of virtually all consumer goods. The industrial power of Great Britain focused on producing war materials. So many commodities that had flowed to Great Britain from its worldwide empire for over a century were in scarce supply because of the German attack on shipping. A meal with any kind of meat came to be a rare occasion. In April 1940, Jack wrote to Warnie that war seemed more remote at Magdalen than at the Kilns because of "the luxury, the shaded candles, the wine, the saddle of mutton, and the conversations about routine matters."[58] By August, however, he wrote that the table at Magdalen College had begun to suffer, the number of courses at dinner had been reduced, and "the idea of Magdalen, of all places, doing that is the most genuinely alarming piece of war news I have heard since the surrender of France."[59] On one occasion, Lewis waited until after the Inklings broke up at nearly 1:00 in the morning to eat the simple sandwich he had for supper because he did not have enough for all and he did not want to eat in front of the others. By 1943, they were keeping rabbits and chickens at the Kilns.

Perhaps the worst shortage of all for the Inklings came when the Eagle and Child ran out of beer and had to close. When this disaster occurred, the group settled in at the White Horse next to Blackwell's Bookshop or the King's Arms, where Broad Street meets Holywell.

Above: The grave of Charles Williams in St. Cross churchyard

Opposite page: After Jack Lewis began to correspond with Sister Penelope, he lectured from time to time at the convent of St. Mary in Wantage, some fifteen miles southwest of Oxford.

THE INKLINGS AND WOMEN

When the Inklings first went up to Oxford as undergraduates, a man could live and teach there for years without the necessity of having any contact with a woman. Of course, change was in the wind even in those last days of empire before the devastation of the Great War. On the fringes of the city, like armed camps laying siege, a ring of new women's colleges had sprung up. The city was surrounded, so it was only a matter of time: St. Anne's, Somerville, St. Hugh's, St. Hilda's, and later St. Catherine's. Many people think that the Inklings lived and worked as though

The front quad of Merton College

The chapel of Merton College

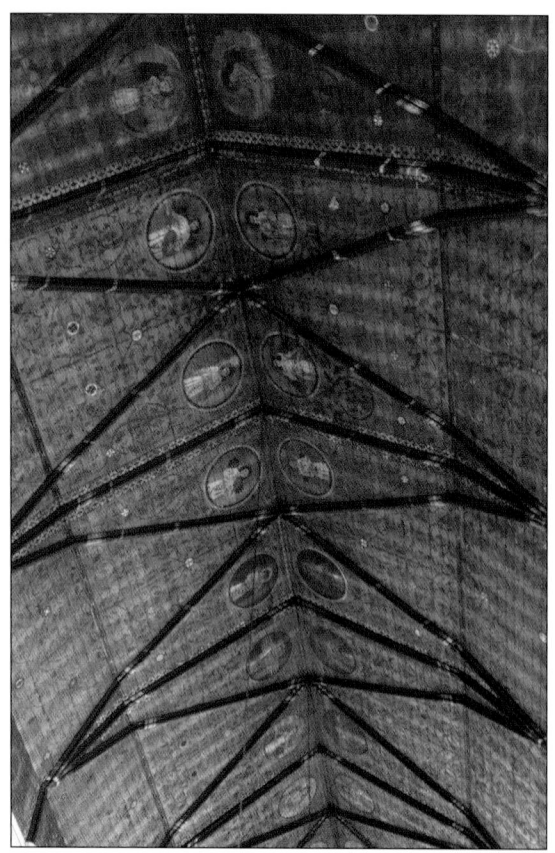

Merton chapel possesses a rare painted ceiling.

the great change had not begun, but they were actually part of the change.

Warnie Lewis may have never learned to talk with ladies, but Charles Williams had mastered the art. In London he had a huge following of female admirers and disciples. After his popular books began coming out, Jack Lewis discovered that he had a large following among women as well. Unlike Williams, who encouraged his following, Lewis left matters at a polite and brief response to letters. With Dorothy L. Sayers, however, Lewis wrote as if writing to a man, which is to say he respected her intellect. Sayers was born in Oxford, where her father directed the choir at Christ Church Cathedral. She belonged to Somerville College and graduated just before the outbreak of World War I. When she first wrote to Lewis, Sayers had the greater reputation. The creator of the Lord Peter Wimsey detective series, Sayers stopped writing detective fiction when her royalties insured her an income that would not require her ever to work again. She then turned her attention to Christian apologetics. After T. S. Eliot and Charles Williams had written the first two plays for the Canterbury Festival (*Murder in the Cathedral* and *Thomas Cranmer of Canterbury*), Dorothy L. Sayers was the obvious choice to write the third. She wrote *The Zeal of Thy House* for the 1937 production, which concerned the rebuilding of the choir of Canterbury Cathedral after a fire in the twelfth century. In this play, she was interested in exploring the relationship between a craftsman and his work, especially as it relates to the fine line between pride in a job well done and pride in oneself. In 1939 she returned with a second play, *The Devil to Pay*, which involved a retelling of the story of Faust and his bargain with the Devil.

Sayers wrote essays and gave public lectures on the proper Christian response to the crisis of war. She wrote a nativity play, *He That Should Come*, for the BBC in 1939. She also wrote a serial drama broadcast over the BBC from December 1941 through October 1942 on the life of Christ that was called *The Man Born to Be King*, which Lewis and Tolkien admired. In addition to the plays and essays, she wrote a book of apologetics, *The Mind of the Maker*, in 1941.

Sayers had met Williams once before the war, but they became friends when she stayed with the Spaldings on one of her numerous visits to Oxford during the war. At first, the highly successful Sayers advised Williams on how to market his books, but in the end she went away smitten by Williams. She read his study of Dante, *The Figure of Beatrice*, and found a new interest that would result in her translation, after the war, of Dante's *Divine Comedy*, though she first had to teach herself Italian!

Other women trod the margins of the Inkling as well. After the publication of *Out of the Silent Planet*, Lewis received a letter of appreciation from Sister Penelope, an Anglican nun of the Community of St. Mary the Virgin in Wantage. This letter began a friendship that would last until Lewis died. She enlisted Lewis to give regular lectures at her convent, and he wrote the introduction to her translation of *The Incarnation of the Word of God* by Athanasius. Lewis dedicated *Perelandra* (1943) to the sisters.

Probably no group of people in the English-speaking world knew more about poetry than the Inklings. Almost all of them wrote poetry. Almost

Detail of the painted ceiling in Merton chapel

The hall at Merton where Tolkien and Dyson often invited their fellow Inklings to dine

Above: Tolkien's rooms at Merton were in the right corner of the Fellows Quad above the door of staircase 4.

Previous page: In 1945 Tolkien was elected Merton Professor of English Literature, which also involved a fellowship at Merton College.

The Inklings frequently met at Tolkien's rooms in Merton after the war.

all of them published poetry. Nonetheless, Jack Lewis knew there was a difference between a person who writes poetry and a poet. The Inklings were not poets. The rational Lewis had given up his own deep ambition to make his mark as a great poet, but somewhere within him, Lewis still longed to achieve something as a poet. He continued to read his poetry at gatherings of the Inklings, but he turned elsewhere for advice on how to write better poetry. He turned to Ruth Pitter, an accomplished and recognized poet who still wrote in traditional forms.

Ruth Pitter had published four volumes of poetry by the beginning of the war, including *Persephone in Hades* (1931), *A Mad Lady's Garland* (1934), *A Trophy of Arms: Poems 1926 – 35* (1936), and *The Spirit Watches* (1939). She had won the Hawthornden Prize in 1937. Living in London, she was one of the literary friends of Lord David Cecil. She and a friend had established a successful business making painted furniture and hand-painted decorator items, but the coming of the war wiped them out, and they went to work in a factory. In 1941 Cecil showed some of her poetry to Lewis. In a letter to Pitter, Cecil said that Lewis "was deeply struck & went off to buy your poems."[60] Pitter in turn wrote to Cecil in 1942 that *The Screwtape Letters* had "excited me more than anything has done for a long time."[61] Pitter's miserable situation in life, however, dragged her downward until she heard Lewis's broadcast talks on the BBC. Through his reasoned approach to faith, Pitter soon converted to Christianity. She became Lewis's friend in 1946 when her friend Herbert Palmer wrote to Lewis asking if he would meet Ruth Pitter. Palmer also encouraged Pitter to write to Lewis about a meeting. Lewis immediately replied and invited Pitter to visit him that very week.

In October 1946, Jack invited Ruth Pitter to lunch at Magdalen College. He was

Above: The Tolkiens lived at 3 Manor Road near St. Cross Church from 1947 until 1950.

Below: Warnie Lewis enjoyed the walk from Merton to Magdalen that went along the back of Merton beside the playing field. Merton incorporated a section of the old city wall as the back wall of the college.

When Dyson received his appointment as fellow at Merton College, he and his wife moved to 12 Holywell Street.

(Photo by Rebecca Whitten Poe)

having "a few people." He mentioned the Cecils, whom Ruth knew. He added that Dyson spoke of her poetry "with something like awe" and that he wanted to meet her. The luncheon was held in the New Room. In his diary, Warnie mentioned sitting next to Ruth Pitter at the "mixed lunch" that Jack had given. Warnie did not write more because Jack Lewis was not in the habit of giving "mixed lunches" where men brought their wives. After dining with a couple one night, Lewis had written to Warnie that a meeting with a friend and the rest of his family "is always partly a meeting wasted."[62]

PEACE AND CHANGE

The war in Europe ended officially on May 9, 1945. Charles Williams died the following Tuesday on May 15. Ironically, it was the morning on which the Inklings gathered at the Eagle and Child, and Jack went straight from the hospital to the Eagle and Child to tell the other Inklings the bad news. In his diary, Warnie Lewis lamented, "There will be no more pints with Charles: no more 'Bird and Baby': the blackout has fallen, and the Inklings can never be the same again."[63] The Inklings would not be the same, but not simply because Williams had died. Whenever a person leaves a circle of friends, and whenever a new person enters that circle, the dynamic changes. Tolkien might just as easily have written in 1939 when Williams joined the group that the Inklings could never be the same again. Other people and their lives contributed to the change the Inklings would undergo over the next few years.

Though Hugo Dyson had actively participated in Inklings gatherings throughout the 1930s, he had lived the entire time in Reading, where he taught at Reading University. Throughout the war he continued to travel to Oxford to be with his friends, but in 1945 he

In the opposite direction from Tolkien's house, Dyson could see the King's Arms from his front door to the right at the west end of Holywell Street.

received an appointment as Fellow and Lecturer in English Literature at Merton College. He and his wife, Margaret, took a house at 12 Holywell Street, near New College and Magdalen. The Dysons had no children, but they had a notoriously happy marriage. Even confirmed bachelors like Jack Lewis had to acknowledge their appreciation for Margaret. After staying overnight once with the Dysons in Reading, Lewis wrote, "Rare luck to stay with a friend whose wife is so nice that one *almost* (I can't say quite) *almost* regrets the change when he takes you up to his study for serious smoking and for the real midnight talking."[64] Dyson clearly enjoyed a different kind of domestic experience from Jack Lewis.

Dyson had faithfully attended Inklings meetings when he lived twenty-five miles away, but moving to Oxford changed his pattern of life. It would no longer be as easy to get to Jack's room on a Thursday night. As long as Dyson's Oxford friends were collected together in one room in Magdalen College, he had no difficulty going straight to the meeting. Once he became a part of the Oxford scene, however, his natural gregariousness made it difficult for him to move from point A to point B without striking up two or three new friendships. In August 1946, Warnie described Dyson's problem in his diary: "I saw tonight why Hugo rarely gets to an Inkling; every one he meets after dinner he engages in earnest conversation, and tonight, even with steady pressure from me, it took him 40 minutes to get from Hall to the gate.... [Finally] we went on to Magdalen, where there was a well attended Inklings."[65] After the war the Inklings often met in Tolkien's rooms at Merton College, where Dyson had his fellowship. Warnie wrote in his diary that as he arrived at Merton for an Inklings, he could hear Dyson's booming voice inviting a group of undergraduates up to his rooms. Warnie noted that Dyson could "be very irritating at times."[66]

Change also came to Tolkien, who had gone up to Oxford in 1925 as the Professor of Anglo-Saxon. One professorship in a lifetime is more than most Oxford fellows ever have, but in 1945

Gervase Mathew, a Byzantine scholar who took the initiative in becoming an Inkling, was a member of the Dominican Order at Blackfriars in St. Giles.

St. John's College provided a research fellowship to John Wain who became one of the new young members of the Inklings after the war.

The garden of New College includes a large section of the original city wall of Oxford that dates to the twelfth century.

Tolkien was elected Merton Professor of English Language and Literature at the same time Hugo Dyson was elected a fellow of Merton College. The new post also involved a move from Pembroke College, an old but poor establishment, to Merton College, a rather elegant place. It also meant that Tolkien enjoyed a status that Jack and Hugo did not enjoy in a status-conscious society. In addition to the status of a second professorship came the financial benefit of a more prestigious professorship. The Tolkien family lodgings reflected the rise in Tolkien's earnings. When Tolkien came to Oxford in 1925, the family had a house in North Oxford at 22 Northmoor Road. In 1930 they moved to the larger house next door at 20 Northmoor Road. With the Merton Professorship, and without a house full of children, however, Tolkien moved to a smaller house at 3 Manor Road near St. Cross Church. Jack Lewis hoped that he might gain a professorship in 1946 when David Nichol Smith retired as Professor of English Literature. Tolkien considered Lewis's chances hopeless, so he supported their friend Lord David Cecil for the post, but neither Inkling was elected. The chair went to Lewis's old tutor, F. P. Wilson. In 1948, however, Lord David joined Tolkien with a professorship as Goldsmiths Professor of English Literature.

Nevill Coghill, who had introduced Jack Lewis to Hugo Dyson, helped him publish *Dymer*, and persuaded him to read his first book by Charles Williams, had been a central figure in the Inklings since its beginning, but his other interests increasingly ate into his discretionary time. Coghill proved to have a talent for producing plays. He devoted more and more of his time to drama. He wrote plays and directed plays. As a result, Coghill rarely came to the Inklings gatherings after the war. When the Princess Elizabeth visited Oxford University on May 25, 1948, the entire university rose to the occasion with banquets, receptions, and the full range of ceremony that the combined resources of the monarchy and the university could muster. Jack Lewis wrote to Dr. Warfield Firor, an American admirer, about the looming spectacle of "lunches, teas, dinners, visits to various dignitaries, and an open air play," but added that he would "escape with a play and a garden party."[67] Coghill wrote and produced the play, entitled *The Masque of Hope*, given in honor of Princess Elizabeth.

Warfield Firor had made the postwar gloom of Oxford somewhat brighter for the Inklings because of his habit of sending hams and other luxurious gifts to Jack. The end of the war had not meant an end to shortages. From 1945 until 1950 the nation struggled out of the wreckage of war. Whenever Jack received a ham, he hosted a grand dinner party for the Inklings at Magdalen. These ham suppers became a special delight when food was still scarce.

The end of the war also brought new friends into the Inklings. Christopher Tolkien became the youngest and one of the most faithful members when he returned from the war. Jack Lewis brought several members of Magdalen College along to the Inklings meetings. Colin Hardie, with whom Jack Lewis had been reading Dante, was invited to attend. In 1946, Charles Wrenn returned to Oxford, after a sojourn at King's College, London, to take up Tolkien's old place as Professor of Anglo-Saxon. C. E. Stevens, who tutored in Ancient History, and J. A. W. Bennett, who tutored in Anglo-Saxon, also became members. Gervase Mathew, a Dominican who resided at Blackfriars, invited himself into the circle and became faithful in attendance. John Wain, a former student of Jack Lewis, was invited to attend Inklings meetings soon after the war, but his outlook on almost every matter differed significantly from the views of the older Inklings. In a letter to his

Lewis spent many hours in the Bodleian Library after the war while working on his *English Literature in the Sixteenth Century*.

Above: Antony Flew, premier defender of atheism in the twentieth century, belonged to the Socratic Club and attended the Lewis-Anscombe debate. (Photo by Ben Dockery)

Opposite page: Lewis returned to Magdalen College across Magdalen Bridge after his debate with Elizabeth Anscombe at St. Hilda's College.

son Christopher during the war, Tolkien had mentioned a wonderful morning at the Eagle and Child with Jack, Warnie, and Charles Williams, but said that he could "recollect little of the feast of reason and flow of soul, partly because we agree so."[68] As old friends left and new friends came into the Inklings, this kind of agreement began to change.

DISCOURAGEMENT AND SUCCESS

For years, Tolkien had devoted his free time to writing a history of the mythic world of Middle Earth. Notoriously precise in his details, Tolkien was known to rewrite huge passages of text to make the phases of the moon come out right. Dyson tired of hearing tales of elves and hobbits after the war, so Tolkien stopped reading his "New Hobbit" at Inklings gatherings when Dyson came. Furthermore, the last part of the Lord of the Rings did not come easily to Tolkien, and this was not the first time he had stalled. He had gone for almost a year in 1940 without writing. Again in 1944 he stalled for months, but when his son joined the RAF and went to South Africa for training, he resumed writing and told Christopher about it in his letters. He was reading the new installments to

Derek Brewer, for many years Master of Emmanuel College of Cambridge University, dined with Lewis and Dyson a few days after the Lewis-Anscombe debate.

Jack, Warnie, and Charles Williams at the White Horse.[69] He also continued to read to Jack Lewis on their Monday morning meetings, which had predated the founding of the Inklings. In 1945, however, Tolkien wrote very little. In 1947, he began one more push, but he did not finally complete the manuscript until 1949, when he was almost sixty years old.

For Jack Lewis, the end of the war meant freedom from his war work. He declined an invitation to speak further on the BBC. He had his unfinished manuscript in the Oxford History of the English Language series gathering dust. He had several projects begun during the war that needed completion. He had written a third science-fiction book in his Ransom series that brought events back to earth in *That Hideous Strength*. In this tale he explored the corrupting influence of cliques that pursue power which he dubbed "the inner ring," while raising the ethical dilemmas of scientific experimentation on humans.

In 1943 he began a book about miracles that was not published until 1947. In *Miracles* Lewis explored the fundamental logical fallacies of a materialistic worldview and the idea that everything simply arose by chance. On February 2, 1948, at a public meeting of the Socratic Club, Elizabeth Anscombe presented a paper that criticized a chapter from *Miracles* that explored how naturalism refutes itself. Simply stated, Lewis had laid out Charles Darwin's great horror about the Theory of Natural Selection: "No thought is valid if it can be fully explained as the result of irrational causes."[70] As such, human reason cannot make truth claims about naturalism or anything else. Anscombe, a disciple of Ludwig Wittgenstein and his Linguistic Analysis school of philosophy, focused her criticism on the different meanings of "cause" and "because." This was a different way of doing philosophy than Lewis had learned in his undergraduate days. Anscombe had also mastered the theatrical techniques of public debate and puffed on a cigar while Lewis attempted to answer her charges. Lewis left the meeting dejected, feeling he had lost the debate, but more importantly, feeling that his loss had opened doubts in the minds of others.

Two days later at a supper club dinner with Hugo Dyson and four students, Derek Brewer, Peter Bayley, Philip Stibbe, and Tom Stock, Lewis described the Anscombe encounter with the imagery of the "fog of war." By Derek Brewer's account, Lewis was deeply disturbed, and Dyson finally said, "Very well – that now he had lost everything and was come to the foot of the cross...."[71] Hugo Dyson told the story to other students. John Lucas, who taught philosophy at Oxford for many years, recalls that Dyson "used to say that Lewis had said words to the effect 'It shows that I am no philosopher,' to which Dyson replied 'We never thought you were, Jack: you are a literary man.'"[72] Discussion continues to rage over whether Lewis "lost" the debate with Anscombe. Those close to Lewis have reported that he thought he had lost and subsequently revised chapter three of *Miracles* to meet Anscombe's objections. Lucas and Basil Mitchell, who succeeded Lewis as president of the Socratic Club and held the Noleth Chair of Christian Philosophy at Oxford for many years, offer another interpretation. They insist that Lewis had the stronger argument and that his reasoning presents a strong critique of the problems with naturalism. On the other hand, Anscombe had the "gamesmanship" and bullying tricks that enabled her to put on the winning show. In short, Anscombe won the public debate, but Lewis had the winning argument.

As the privations of postwar Britain began to ease, and the climate of the country changed, the Inklings continued to face even more changes. A new chapter in the life of the Inklings came in 1949. In his diary entry for October 20, 1949, Warnie noted that no one came for the Inklings meeting that night, "which was just as well, as J has had a bad cold and wanted to go to bed early."[73] The Inklings would never again meet for a Thursday night gathering in Jack's rooms in Magdalen. They would still have the Tuesday mornings at the Eagle and Child, but an important phase in their friendship had passed away.

Basil Mitchell, for many years Noleth Professor of Christian Philosophy at Oxford, succeeded Lewis as president of the Socratic Club. He has said that Elizabeth Anscombe was a master at the kind of "gamesmanship" that might have won the debate with Lewis, but that Lewis had the stronger argument.

FOUR

"LIVING TILL WE DIE"

With the last of his "war works" out of the way, Lewis turned his attention to the kind of writing he preferred: one full of fancy and imagination. He decided to write a children's story. He actually started the story at the beginning of the war when one of the girls who had been evacuated to the Kilns asked if she could go inside one of the numerous wardrobes to see if there was anything behind it. He had also had a picture in his mind since the age of sixteen of a fawn carrying packages and an umbrella in the snow. Not until 1948, however, did he finally finish a draft of *The Lion, the Witch and the Wardrobe* over Christmas break. When he read it to Tolkien, he was distressed by the reaction. Tolkien hated it. Lewis had mixed up mythological figures from a variety of times and cultures. It violated Tolkien's sense of order. Fawns were fine in their place, but not in a story that included Father Christmas.

Above: From his front door at 12 Holywell Street, Hugo Dyson could see Tolkien's house at the end of the street on the right.

Following page: New College where Christopher Tolkien held a fellowship.

Opposite page: Near Parson's Pleasure where Lewis loved to swim stands an oddly isolated lamppost like the one Lucy found in Narnia.

Above: The Tolkiens moved to 76 Sandfield Road in Headington where they lived from 1953 until 1968.

Below: The Tolkiens attended the Catholic Church of Corpus Christi in Headington at the corner of Margaret Road and Wharton Road.

Fortunately, Lewis did not leave it there. Others encouraged him to publish the story. He sent it to Geoffrey Bles, his publisher, but their view was that a children's story by C. S. Lewis would not sell unless it was part of a series. So, Lewis set out to write an entire series of the Chronicles of Narnia. Thus, Lewis, who had seemingly dashed off his mythological story, found a publisher eager to print not only what Tolkien considered an inferior work, but also an entire series of unwritten books, while Tolkien still searched for someone to publish the Lord of the Rings.

When Jack Lewis first moved in with Mrs. Moore after World War I, they took care of each other. By the beginning of World War II, Jack took

The interior of Corpus Christi

care of Mrs. Moore. By the end of the war, however, this care had become a great burden. In addition, Warnie struggled with alcoholism that could send him on long drinking bouts that only ended when he was admitted to hospital. Mrs. Moore's varicose veins had troubled her for years, but they made walking almost impossible by war's end. One reason Jack wrote less during the years that followed the war was that his domestic situation prevented it. In January 1950, however, Mrs. Moore fell from bed three times in one night. She was taken to Rest-holme, a nursing home where Warnie had already spent time when recovering from his drinking bouts. Today she might be diagnosed as suffering from Alzheimer's disease, for she went from childish or incoherent moods to moods of anger. She died of influenza in January of the following year. Warnie wrote in his diary of her death: "And so ends the mysterious self imposed slavery in which J has lived for at least thirty years."[74] For Warnie, it meant he finally had his best friend back.

Mrs. Moore's death came right in the middle of the election campaigning for the Chair of Poetry which had fallen vacant again. This time Jack's name was on the list. His opponent was Cecil Day Lewis, who had written several volumes of poetry,

A detail of J. R. R. Tolkien and Hugo Dyson, taken from a photograph of the faculty of Merton College in 1954, the year that *The Fellowship of the Ring* was published (From the collection of Harry Lee Poe)

J. R. R. Tolkien seated beneath a tree in the gardens of Merton College (© Copyright by Billett Potter, Oxford)

including *Transition Poems*, *Magnetic Mountain*, *A Time for Dance*, *Short Is the Time*, and *Poems 1943 – 1947*. Jack Lewis had managed to make his share of enemies over the years, not least of which for his management of Adam Fox's election as Professor of Poetry on the grounds that the post should go to a practicing poet. The opposition borrowed Jack Lewis's earlier strategy, insisting that C. Day Lewis *was* the practicing poet this time. C. Day Lewis could also rely upon what Warnie called the "Atheist-Communist bloc." A ballot with the names C. D. Lewis and C. S. Lewis added to the drama, but in the end Jack lost by a vote of 194 to 173. Never again would Jack's name be proposed for a professorship at Oxford.

With an end to the evening gatherings of the Inklings, the Tuesday morning times at the Eagle and Child became the focus of Inkling activity rather than the adjunct they had once been.

TOLKIEN AND THE LORD OF THE RINGS

With the new decade, more changes came for the Inklings. The Tolkiens moved from their small house on Manor Road

The Lewis brothers went to St. Peter's-in-the-East on Wednesday mornings for Communion. The church has now been turned into a library for St. Edmund Hall.

to a larger and more prestigious residence owned by Merton College at 99 Holywell. Whereas the children's books of Jack Lewis would come out one a year at Christmastime beginning in 1950, Tolkien still had no publisher for the Lord of the Rings. Negotiations dragged on first with Sir Stanley Unwin, then with Milton Waldman of Collins, then back to Unwin. Months stretched into years until finally in November 1952, Unwin agreed to publish. The publishers recognized the literary achievement of the book and thought it deserved publication, but they regarded it as that sort of book that sees print as a duty to the profession rather than as a way to make money. Instead of offering Tolkien an advance and a royalty, Unwin offered Tolkien an equal share in the profits once the expenses of publication were covered. It was a good business decision for Unwin, if he had judged the market correctly, because it meant he would never pay

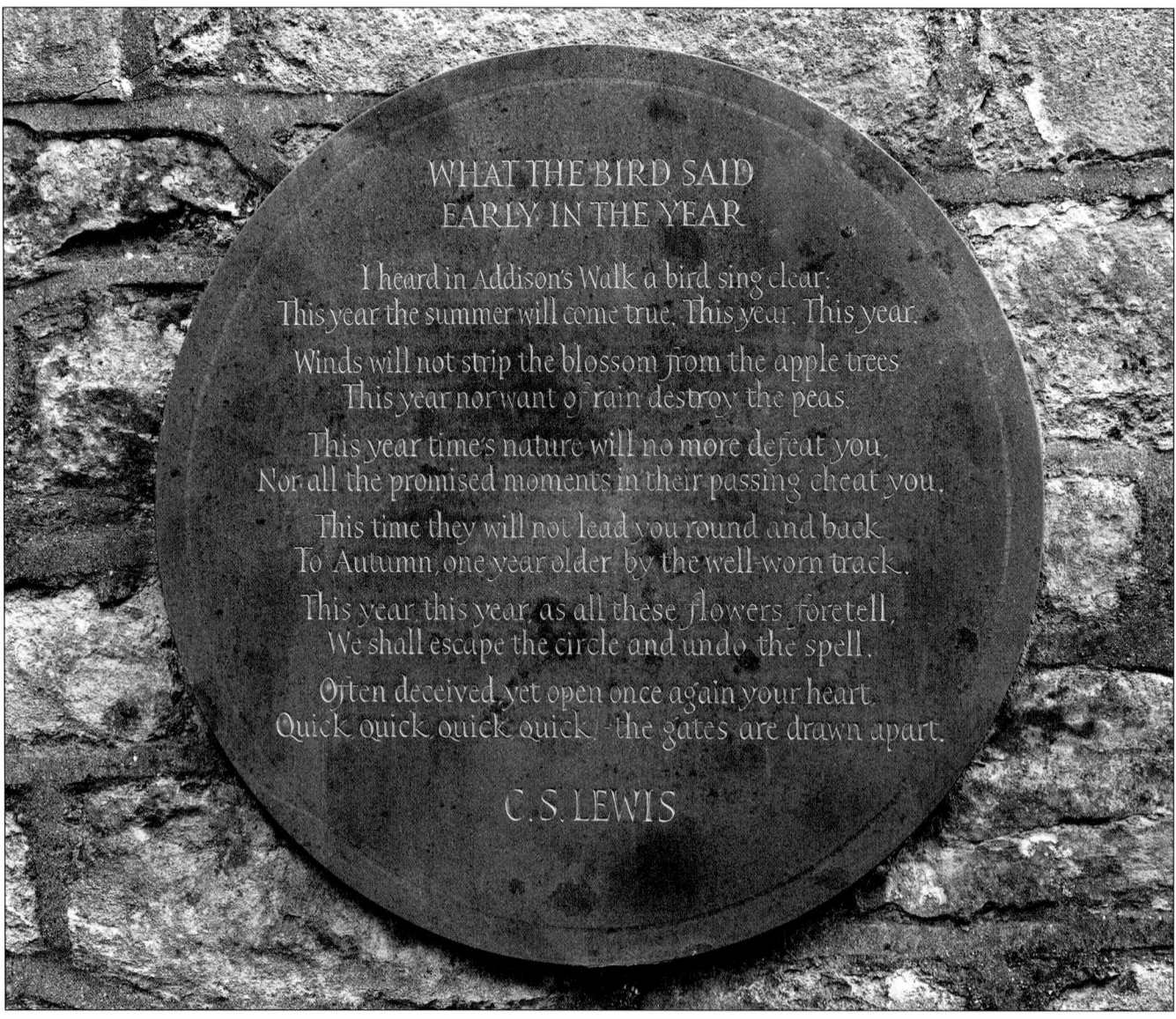

Above: Magdalen College, Oxford, has commemorated the life of Jack Lewis by placing a plaque in Addison's Walk that contains a poem he wrote the year before he died, "What the Bird Said Early in the Year."

Previous page: In 1954 Jack Lewis bade farewell to his rooms in the New Building of Magdalen College.

![Magdalene College, Cambridge exterior with person on bicycle]

Magdalene College, Cambridge, is not as large and grand as Magdalen College, Oxford, but Lewis found a ready home there.

Tolkien a farthing. In a world where it is normally safe to underestimate the taste of the reading public, however, Unwin's judgment proved wrong. An equal share in the profits turned out to be a good arrangement for Tolkien due to the books' success.

Despite the charm and prestige of the Holywell residence, the Tolkiens grew tired of the hustle and bustle of traffic in town. They decided to move again in 1953 to 76 Sandfield Road in Headington not far from the Kilns. In August 1954, the first volume of the Lord of the Rings finally appeared in print. Jack Lewis did all he could to promote the book, writing in a review of the book for *Time & Tide*, "This book is like lightning from a clear sky."[75] His view turned out to be more than mere enthusiasm for his friend's work. Tolkien's story of the ring of power and those who banded together to destroy it soon became a popular sensation, especially among

First Court of Magdalene College looking toward the hall from the porter's lodge.

The small dining room beneath Lewis's rooms with the table set for dinner

Previous page: Lewis's rooms stretched along the upper level above the small dining room in First Court.

Above: Lewis joined Simon Barrington-Ward, the chaplain of Magdalene College, every morning he was in Cambridge for morning prayer in the chapel, where he always sat in the rear corner facing the altar.

college students. He resisted the idea of a paperback edition until 1965 when Ace Books produced a pirated edition in the United States.

Once the Lord of the Rings came out in paperback, Tolkien became a cult phenomenon on college campuses. The generation that protested everything from the war in Vietnam to the pollution of the environment found something in the struggle of the hobbits against the Dark Lord for which they longed. A cultural conservative and pious Catholic, Tolkien did not write a tale to overthrow the social order but to restore what was lost. Along with the flower children of the 1960s, young Christians of all stripes from evangelical to Catholic found common ground in the story of the Ring. On the surface, the story does not seem particularly Christian. It does not mention God, nor does it give an explanation of how to go to heaven when you die, a necessary ingredient for much that passes for "Christian fiction."

The underlying faith of Tolkien shines throughout the story in the attitudes of the hobbits, but we see it clearly if we compare Tolkien's story of the ring of power with the same story as told by Richard Wagner in his four epic operas that make up *The Ring of the Niebelungen*. Of course, Tolkien resented the suggestion that he had simply copied Wagner's story and insisted, "Both rings were round, and there the resemblance ceased."[76]

In the Lord of the Rings Tolkien constructed a fabulous myth. We find the universal story of the dying and rising figure with Gandalf, who certainly dies and goes down to the pit, but who comes back again changed. We also find the story of the "return of the king." The return of the king is an ancient Christian idea, and the king who returns is the Lord Jesus Christ. Ever since the resurrection of Jesus, the king who returns has figured prominently in such stories as King Arthur. You remember that King Arthur went across the waters to Avalon, and that he shall return one day when Britain is in dire trouble and rescue the land. In the early days of the Christian Roman Empire, around the year 360, a group of stories appeared known as the Sibylline Oracles. During this period there was a relapse to paganism, and the Sibylline Oracles told that the great and true Christian emperor would return at the last times. The whole idea of the return of the king is deeply rooted in medieval Christian understanding. Tolkien also explains what kind of world we have with Middle Earth. Tolkien provided the background for the events in the Lord of the Rings in another book called *The Silmarillion*. There he describes the origin of Middle Earth and everything else:

> There was Eru, the One, who in Arda is called Ilúvatar; and he made first the Ainur, the Holy Ones, that were the offspring of his thought, and they were with him before aught else was made. And he spoke to them themes of music; and they sang before him, and he was glad. But for a long while they sang only each alone, or but few together, while the rest hearkened; for each comprehended only that part of the mind of Ilúvatar from which he came, and in the understanding of their brethren they grew but slowly. Yet ever as they listened they came to deeper understanding, and increased in unison and harmony.
>
> And it came to pass that Ilúvatar called together all the Ainur and declared to them a mighty theme, unfolding to them things greater and more wonderful than he had yet revealed; and the glory of its beginning and the splendour of its end amazed the Ainur, so that they bowed before Ilúvatar and were silent.[77]

Here unfolds the doctrine of creation by the One, the creator God, who conceives all things and brings them to pass through his thought and through his will. This is the kind of world Tolkien has created.

The Norse ring legend looks quite different from a pagan perspective. Richard Wagner set it to music in *The Ring of the Neibelungen*, which tells the story of the dwarf, Albriech, who renounced love, stole the Rhine Maidens' gold, and fashioned a ring through which he controlled all the world: the world of the gods, the world of the giants, the world of the humans, the world of the dwarves under the earth. Wagner's opera cycle is concerned with fate and determinism, while Tolkien

Lewis delivered his inaugural lecture as Professor of Medieval and Renaissance Literature in the Mill Lane Lecture Hall in Cambridge.

Barbara Reynolds, the great Dante scholar, represented her friend Dorothy L. Sayers at Lewis's inaugural address in Cambridge as Professor of Medieval and Renaissance Literature.

Joy Gresham and her two sons lived at 10 Old High Street in Headington before they moved to the Kilns.

extols freedom and free will. Wagner preaches nihilism and futility. At the end of his opera, Siegfried lies dead, Brunhilda kills herself, and Valhalla, the dwelling place of the gods, is consumed in flames. At the end of Tolkien's story, however, the weak have overcome the strong, evil is destroyed, and harmony is restored to Middle Earth by a selfless, sacrificial act. The motivation for Wagner's hero, Siegfried, is vanity and pride. Tolkien's hero, Frodo, is motivated by self-sacrifice rooted in love for others. Siegfried has arrogance, but Frodo has humility. With Siegfried the underlying theme is sex, but with Frodo the underlying theme is love.

LEWIS GOES TO CAMBRIDGE

C. S. Lewis wrote the seven books that made up the Chronicles of Narnia with little effort in short periods of time. Other than his children's books and an edited compilation of his BBC talks that were issued under the title *Mere Christianity*, Lewis avoided any other projects until he completed his volume for the Oxford History of English Literature. It was published at the Clarendon Press in 1954 as *English Literature in the Sixteenth Century, Excluding Drama*, a massive scholarly achievement that is still highly regarded fifty years later. One might have thought that with this volume, a professorship would surely come. It did, but not in the way that anyone would have expected. Cambridge University offered Lewis its newly created Professorship of Medieval and Renaissance Literature and a fellowship at Magdalene College.

Besides the disappointment over losing one professorship after another, Lewis had other reasons to consider a move. The English faculty had changed, and ideas about what should be taught changed as well. He had followed Tolkien's leadership twenty

Above: The chapel of Trinity College where Austin Farrer served for many years as chaplain and where Christopher Tolkien was an undergraduate

years earlier in restricting instruction to literature before the Victorian period with an emphasis on Old English. Lord David Cecil, however, wrote and studied extensively on the Victorian period. Tolkien served on the committee that recommended extending the course of study into the twentieth century, but when it came for a vote of the English faculty, Lewis managed to marshal enough votes to stop it for the time being. Within the English faculty, and even within his own college, Lewis did not feel as though he had a place. In a note to his former student Emrys Jones, who succeeded him as a fellow in English at Magdalen College when he left for Cambridge, Lewis wrote, "Magdalen SCR is a dangerous place."[78] At Oxford, the SCR, or Senior Common Room, is the comfortable lounge near the dining hall in each college where faculty members gather to relax

Above: Joy Davidman outside the Kilns

(Used by permission of The Marion
E. Wade Center, Wheaton College, Wheaton, IL.)

and talk at tea time and before and after meals. Underneath it all, Oxford was a place unfriendly for Christians. Jack had fought the prejudice for years, but by now he was fifty-five and not in good health. Jack Lewis was tired.

Nonetheless, Jack still had Warnie to consider. They had a home at the Kilns that had become more homey for Warnie since Mrs. Moore's death. It would mean an end to little things, like attending Communion at St. Peter's-in-the-East together on Wednesday mornings. In the end, Jack decided to keep the Kilns and only spend part of each week in Cambridge. As a professor, he did not have the heavy load of tutorials every day that had been his burden for thirty years. The Inklings changed their morning at the Eagle and Child to Mondays, but this meant an end to the private meetings with Tolkien that had formed such an important part of their friendship. In those days it was still possible, but difficult, to take the train from Oxford to Cambridge, which meant that a man like Jack who had never learned to drive could make the trip. Frequently, instead of taking the train, Lewis hired Alfred Morris, an Oxford taxi driver, to drive him to Cambridge, which allowed for stops along the way for picnics or friendly pubs. In Cambridge, he had adequate rooms in Magdalene College where he could live during the week.

The hall of Keble College where Austin Farrer presided and where young Jack Lewis would have eaten with his friend Paddy Moore before they went to war

Following page: The chapel of Keble College from the University Parks Austin Farrer was elected warden of Keble College in 1960.

The 1950s meant a new period of productivity for Warnie. What had begun as a mere diversion for Warnie Lewis during the war had blossomed into a new career for him in the 1950s. The book he wrote on Louis XIV was published in 1953 as *The Splendid Century: Life in the France of Louis XIV.* This book only led him further into his explorations of the era of the Sun King, and in 1955 he published *Sunset of the Splendid Century.* In 1958 he published *Assault on Olympus: The Rise of the House of Gramont Between 1604 and 1678.* The next year he published *Louis XVI: An Informal Portrait.* The publisher did not publish them as a favor to Jack. Indeed, Warnie did not use Jack's publisher. To

The tables of Keble hall set for a proper dinner

Francis Warner, who now holds appointments at Oxford and Cambridge, was Lewis's research student in Cambridge when he worked with T. S. Eliot.

(Photo by Rebecca Whitten Poe)

Nevill Coghill's protégé Richard Burton and Burton's wife, Elizabeth Taylor, starred in Coghill's production of *Dr. Faustus* at the Oxford Playhouse.

write four significant books in a field in one decade is a notable achievement for anyone, but the significance of the achievement is all the more striking, for Warnie researched and wrote while struggling with recurring alcoholic episodes.

When a new person assumes a professorship in a British university, they deliver an inaugural lecture that lays out their interests and concerns for their discipline. On November 29, 1954, Lewis delivered "De Descriptione Temporum" in the Mill Lane lecture hall in Cambridge to a packed house. Dorothy L. Sayers could not attend, but she sent Barbara Reynolds, her young protégé, to hear what Lewis had to say and to report back. In his lecture, Lewis rejected the old system of dividing western history into periods like Classical, Medieval, Renaissance, and Enlightenment. Instead, he argued that the most significant and dramatic change in western civilization occurred between the time of Jane Austen and his day. The modern world was different from the past, but different in a new way. All of the arts had entered an era in which the culture at large did not understand the art produced by the professional poets, formal composers, painters, and sculptors. Machines had changed how people relate to nature and given way to the myth that the new is better because it is new. Lewis said that in many ways he was a dinosaur, a relic of the past, Old Western Man.

TWICE SURPRISED BY JOY

Lewis had spent the odd hour since 1948 reflecting on his life as he wrote a spiritual autobiography, a less obscure telling of the same story he had told allegorically in *The Pilgrim's Regress*. He had completed the manuscript by early 1955 and it was published later that year as *Surprised by Joy*. Humphrey Havard quipped in a letter to George Sayer that it might be better named "Suppressed by Jack" because of the omission of so many personal details that people wondered about. Lewis did not aim for the sensational in this devotional classic that has achieved bestseller status. Instead, he focused on the way people search for something when they do not even know what it is they are after. Lewis called this yearning "Joy," but it was the joy of longing rather than the joy of satisfaction. It was the knowledge that whatever it was that he sought must be there to be found. Lewis found that his story was a very old story, not unlike the *Confessions* of Augustine written 1500 years earlier. Lewis found that Christ was what he had been looking for, but he only realized it when he believed.

The Inklings abandoned the Eagle and Child when remodeling changed their back room. A rear view shows how the small pub has grown over the years.

In many ways, the 1950s provided a new beginning to life for C. S. Lewis. Part of him that he had kept packed away during all his years of caring for Mrs. Moore began to come out. While he could write about his love of male company and dissatisfaction with female conversation, his self-perception did not always match the perception of others. Theresa Whistler, one of David Cecil's students who later worked for him as his secretary after her marriage in 1950, recalled dinner at the Cecils' with Lewis:

> David knew I admired C. S. Lewis greatly, as he did. I went to every lecture: to his electrifying University Sermon on the afterlife, and to the Socratic debating society where he beat down every opponent. But he played so dominant a solo on all these public occasions, that I was taken aback by the man who came to dinner. In the atmosphere David and Rachel created he sat unassumingly at ease, glad to talk in quartet, all dominance vanished. It was a lively, lovely evening and when he left, on impulse he bent over Rachel's hand and kissed it – the gesture so attractively spontaneous, I wished he would do the same to me![79]

After Mrs. Moore died, Jack Lewis began paying visits to Ruth Pitter, who had moved from London to the village of Long Crendon in Buckinghamshire, the county adjoining Oxforshire to the northeast. His former student and close friend George Sayer drove Lewis to see Pitter on several occasions. Sayer recalled, "It was obvious that he liked her very

When the Inklings left the Eagle and Child, they made their new home at the Lamb and Flag just across the way.

Walter Hooper lived with Lewis and helped with his correspondence the summer before he died.

Jack and Warnie Lewis share a grave stone in Holy Trinity churchyard in Headington.

much. He felt at ease in her presence – and he did not feel relaxed with many people. In fact, he seemed to be on intimate terms with her."[80] After visiting Pitter in 1955, Lewis remarked to Sayer that "if he were not a confirmed bachelor, Ruth Pitter would be the woman he would like to marry."[81] As it was, Lewis did not marry Ruth Pitter because that same year as his remark to George Sayer about marriage, another lady moved to 10 Old High Street in Headington, not far from the Kilns. Her name was Joy Gresham.

Joy Gresham, a native of New York City, had a mystical conversion to faith after an active career in the Communist Party. She had met her husband, Bill Gresham, through the Party in 1942, but after the birth of two children and the events of World War II, they became disillusioned with the Party. Following her conversion, she and Bill studied theology together, and Bill eventually prayed to be released from his alcohol addiction. During this period of early faith, the writings of C. S. Lewis meant a great deal to Joy, who started writing to Lewis in 1950. While Joy grew more committed to her newfound faith, Bill lapsed back into alcoholism and womanizing.

Jack and Joy first met when she visited England in 1952. Lewis had a small luncheon party for her in his rooms at Magdalen College. They were joined by Joy's English pen pal, Phyllis Williams (upon whose invitation she had gone to England), and George Sayer. With his strong prejudice against Americans, it might seem surprising that Jack Lewis would become enchanted by a woman who embodied the caricature of the blunt, abrasive American. Her anti-Americanism, however, far exceeded even Jack's, and he found a kindred spirit.

When Joy returned home, she found her husband and cousin were having an affair. She sued for divorce and returned to England, where she lived in London with her sons, David and Douglas. Joy and her sons spent Christmas 1953 at the Kilns but otherwise had little contact with Lewis until Joy moved to Headington in 1955. The contact they had, however, had consequences. With the Narnia books behind him and his massive study of sixteenth-century English literature published, Jack Lewis needed a new project. Joy encouraged him to write the

Tolkien's grave at Wolvercote Cemetery is frequently decorated by his admirers thirty-five years after his death.

book he had tried and failed to write twice before: a retelling of the myth of Psyche and Cupid, which he called *Till We Have Faces*. The conversation about writing and the encouragement to write now came from a source outside the Inklings. From this point on, Jack's writing depended on Joy much more than it depended upon his old circle of friends.

In 1956 Joy's British residency visa was not renewed, and she had to leave the country unless she married someone with British citizenship. Jack, who had written and taught about courtly love for thirty years, offered to marry Joy in a civil marriage. A civil marriage would provide Joy with the legal protection she needed, but Jack believed it would not violate his understanding of true marriage since it would not be Christian marriage. The marriage was kept secret from all but a few close friends, but Tolkien and the other Inklings were not part of that group. Most of the Inklings and their wives did not care for Joy, with the exception of Charles and Agnes Wrenn. Austin and Katherine Farrer, on the other hand, befriended Joy. Austin Farrer was elected warden of Keble College after many years as chaplain of Trinity College, and Katherine wrote several mystery novels. Jack and Joy continued to live in different houses, and for all the world to see, nothing had changed in their friendship.

Exeter College has commemorated Tolkien by placing in its chapel a bust of him, sculpted by his daughter-in-law.

Dorothy L. Sayers set the marriage of her fictional detective Lord Peter Wimsey at St. Cross Church where Dyson, Williams, and Farrer lie buried.

The grave of Hugo Dyson in St. Cross churchyard

In October 1956 everything changed when Joy fell at home and could not get up. Katherine Farrer arrived at the house upon the intuition that something was wrong and took her to Wingfield Hospital, where they determined that she had cancer. In his diary, Warnie wrote, "I never have loved her more than since she was struck down; her pluck and cheerfulness are beyond praise, and she talks of her disease and its fluctuations as if she was describing the experiences of a friend of hers. God grant that she may recover."[82] As her condition grew worse and death seemed inevitable, Jack's affection grew until he proposed that he and Joy should be married in the eyes of God. On Thursday, March 21, 1957, Joy and Jack married in her hospital room with Peter Bide, one of Jack's former pupils, presiding. To everyone's shock, Joy began to improve. From what Warnie described as her "sentence of death," the cancer went into remission, and Joy came to live at the Kilns.

Finished with his other writing projects, and worried about Joy's health, Lewis began writing a book on the Psalms at Austin Farrer's suggestion. He took on the hard parts that make people uncomfortable. He dealt with the passages that repel modern readers before moving to the passages that bring comfort, hope, and joy. *Reflections on the Psalms* came out in fall 1958. Soon afterward, he was asked by the archbishops of Canterbury and York to serve on the Commission to Revise the Psalter for the Church of England's *Book of Common Prayer*. Among the other six members was his old adversary T. S. Eliot. After nearly forty years of disliking Eliot from a distance for what he had done to modern poetry, Lewis discovered that he liked Eliot and respected his views. Francis Warner, who was Lewis's research student in Cambridge at the time, recalls that, ironically, Eliot pleaded for a more traditional translation of the psalms in the meetings of the commission while Lewis argued for a more contemporary presentation.

About the same time he was involved with the Psalter, Lewis wrote four scripts for radio broadcast in the United

States at the request of the Episcopal Radio-TV Foundation in Atlanta. Allowed to choose his own topic, Lewis chose love. He had addressed a major apologetic issue with *The Problem of Pain* nearly twenty years earlier, but now he took the offensive with the largest problem a convinced materialist had to explain: the problem of love! Love has no place in a purely materialistic/naturalistic world, yet here it is. He recorded these addresses and then used them as the basis for a book, *The Four Loves*, which he published in March 1960.

Joy died the following July.

Following Joy's death, Jack seemed to cope very well. He still went to Cambridge every week. He continued to meet the Inklings for beer and lunch at the Eagle and Child and then across St. Giles at the Lamb and Flag when the Eagle and Child remodeled and changed the back room. He wrote *An Experiment in Criticism*, an important scholarly work on literary criticism, during this period. What no one knew was that he was suffering deep grief and keeping a journal about how he felt. While *The Problem of Pain* provides a rational understanding of the experience of suffering, *A Grief Observed* provides a close encounter with how suffering feels. Lewis published the book under a pseudonym, N. W. Clerk. Even the choice of name was a joke. After Jack realized that he would never be a great poet, he published his poetry in *Punch*, the leading British satirical magazine, under the initials N.W., an abbreviation of *Nat whilk*, which means "I do not know whom" in Anglo-Saxon. Instead of publishing the book with Geoffrey Bles, the publisher with whom he had worked for over twenty years, Lewis published with Faber and Faber where T. S. Eliot held sway.

A popular misconception has grown up among some people, largely due to *Shadowlands*, the film based on the story of Jack and Joy. It creates the impression that Lewis lost his faith. He went through the normal stages of grief that he recorded in *A Grief Observed*, but on the other side of the grief he wrote *Letters to Malcolm Chiefly on Prayer*. It would be his last book, and it was not published until after he died. In the 1940s, Mary Van Deusen, one of his many American correspondents, had suggested that he write a book on prayer. He replied "I don't feel I could write a book on Prayer: I think it would be rather 'cheek' on my part."[83] Not until he had been through the fire with his grief over Joy was Jack ready to write a book on prayer.

Keble College has commemorated the service of Austin Farrer as warden by placing his portrait in the hall.

The narrow entrance to the Eagle and Child

The Eagle and Child remains a favorite pub for the local trade.

Unlike former days, the Eagle and Child is now a favorite place to eat.

THE END OF THE INKLINGS

While Jack Lewis dealt with his grief over Joy's death, Tolkien faced another kind of change in his life. He gave up his professorship and entered retirement. In 1962 he celebrated his seventieth birthday, and his friends contributed essays for a *festshrift* to mark the occasion. He wrote a few more short pieces about Middle Earth and found that he had a public that wanted to know more about him. Articles appeared in major magazines like *The Saturday Evening Post*, and a documentary was produced about him in which he appeared. Hugo Dyson also surprised many by his appearances on the BBC and as an actor in the film *Darling*, which starred Julie Christie in a role for which she won an Oscar.

Nevill Coghill's "producing" of plays, which had kept him from regular attendance at Inklings gatherings for years, led to a screenplay of Marlowe's *Tragical History of Dr. Faustus*, which Richard Burton produced in 1967, codirected with Coghill. It starred Burton and his wife, Elizabeth Taylor, who played Helen of Troy. Coghill also adapted Chaucer's *Canterbury Tales* for a run in the West End of London and on Broadway in 1968. He even wrote the critical introduction to a volume of T. S. Eliot's plays.

Lord David Cecil continued to write on a variety of subjects to great acclaim. He gained additional attention when it became known that John Kennedy ranked Cecil's *The Young Melbourne*, which treated the early career of Lord Melbourne, as one of his favorite books. In 1969 Cecil wrote the introduction to *Ruth Pitter: Homage to a Poet*, which was a collection of essays by prominent literary figures about Pitter and her poetry.

Jack Lewis was never well after Joy's death. He had a variety of ailments about which he did not complain. By 1963, however, he knew that his life as a professor had come

The Tolkiens moved to 99 Holywell Street in 1950 when they found the Manor Road lodgings inadequate.

to an end. He resigned his professorship at Cambridge after a serious heart attack and hospitalization from which the doctors did not believe he would recover. Austin and Katherine Farrer prayed at his bedside while he lay in a coma, and the doctors were surprised that Lewis awoke and asked for tea. Warnie was away on a binge, and a young graduate student from North Carolina agreed to come to the Kilns and help Lewis with his correspondence, the task for which Jack had relied upon Warnie for so many years. Walter Hooper helped Lewis through the summer and went with Lewis to weekly gatherings of the Inklings. He returned to school in the fall when Warnie came home. On November 22, 1963, Lewis died. Few people heard about his death because it was lost in the shocking news of John Kennedy's assassination on the same day. He was buried quietly with a small group of his oldest friends in attendance at Holy Trinity Church in Headington Quarry.

The Inklings made an effort to keep up their meetings at the Lamb and Flag, but it was not the same without Jack Lewis. Hugo Dyson retired the year Jack died. In 1968, Tolkien and his wife, Edith, moved to Bournemouth. In 1969 Charles Wrenn died, and Lord David Cecil retired to his family estate at Cranbourne in Dorset. Colin Hardie retired to Sussex. Humphrey Havard moved to the Isle of Wight. Tolkien moved back to Oxford when Edith died, and he lived in rooms at Merton until his death in 1973, when Warnie and R. B. McCallum also died. Dyson died in 1975, followed by Gervase Mathew and Tom Stevens in 1976.

Christopher Tolkien, who joined the Inklings after his service in World War II, lectured at Oxford and became a fellow of New College in 1963. He has undertaken the enormous task of editing his father's extensive manuscripts about Middle Earth, which have involved over fifteen volumes in thirty years. Walter Hooper attended several Inkling gatherings the summer he lived with Lewis and has devoted his life to the legacy of Lewis's work. These two men are largely responsible for the continuing interest of the broader public in the writings of Lewis and Tolkien.

As for Oxford, the university continues to gather the best and the brightest from around the United Kingdom, the commonwealth, and the world. The students keep the memory of the Inklings alive with the Inklings Society, the C. S. Lewis Society, and the Tolkien Society. Anxious "freshers" still "go up" to Oxford with their ceremonial appearance before the vice chancellor at the Sheldonian Theatre. The old walls and gardens still provide the repose for reflection and good conversation, and in this old city with its dreaming spires, it can still be said,

Your sons and daughters will prophesy,
your young men will see visions,
your old men will dream dreams.

Trepidatious "freshers" enter the gates to the Sheldonian Theatre where they will appear before the Vice Chancellor at matriculation. (Photo by Rebecca Whitten Poe)

APPENDIX: — INKLINGS WALKING — TOURS OF OXFORD

THE CITY OF OXFORD

For those with limited time, the walking tour of the city of Oxford is divided into three parts. Part One includes some of the most familiar Lewis and Tolkien sites. Many of the colleges open for visitors in the afternoons but do not admit visitors in the mornings. If you only have time for Part One, you might want to add a visit to the Eagle and Child in St. Giles to conclude your walking tour.

THE INKLINGS TOUR OF THE CITY OF OXFORD

Walking Tour 1: From Carfax Tower to New College

A walking tour of the Inklings' Oxford begins at one of the city's most prominent landmarks, the Carfax Tower, which stands at the intersection where the High Street meets the Cornmarket, Queen's Street, and St. Aldate's Street. Walk south, down the hill from the Carfax on St. Aldate's Street to St. Aldate's Church, and turn left just past the church. (1) The college across this quiet side street from the church is **Pembroke** ➤, where J. R. R. Tolkien spent twenty years as fellow and Professor of Anglo-Saxon.

Return to St. Aldate's Street and turn right, away from the Carfax. Go one block and turn right onto Brewer Street. (2) The stone house on the left at ◄ **1 Brewer Street** is the house in which Dorothy L. Sayers was born. Return to St. Aldate's and continue one

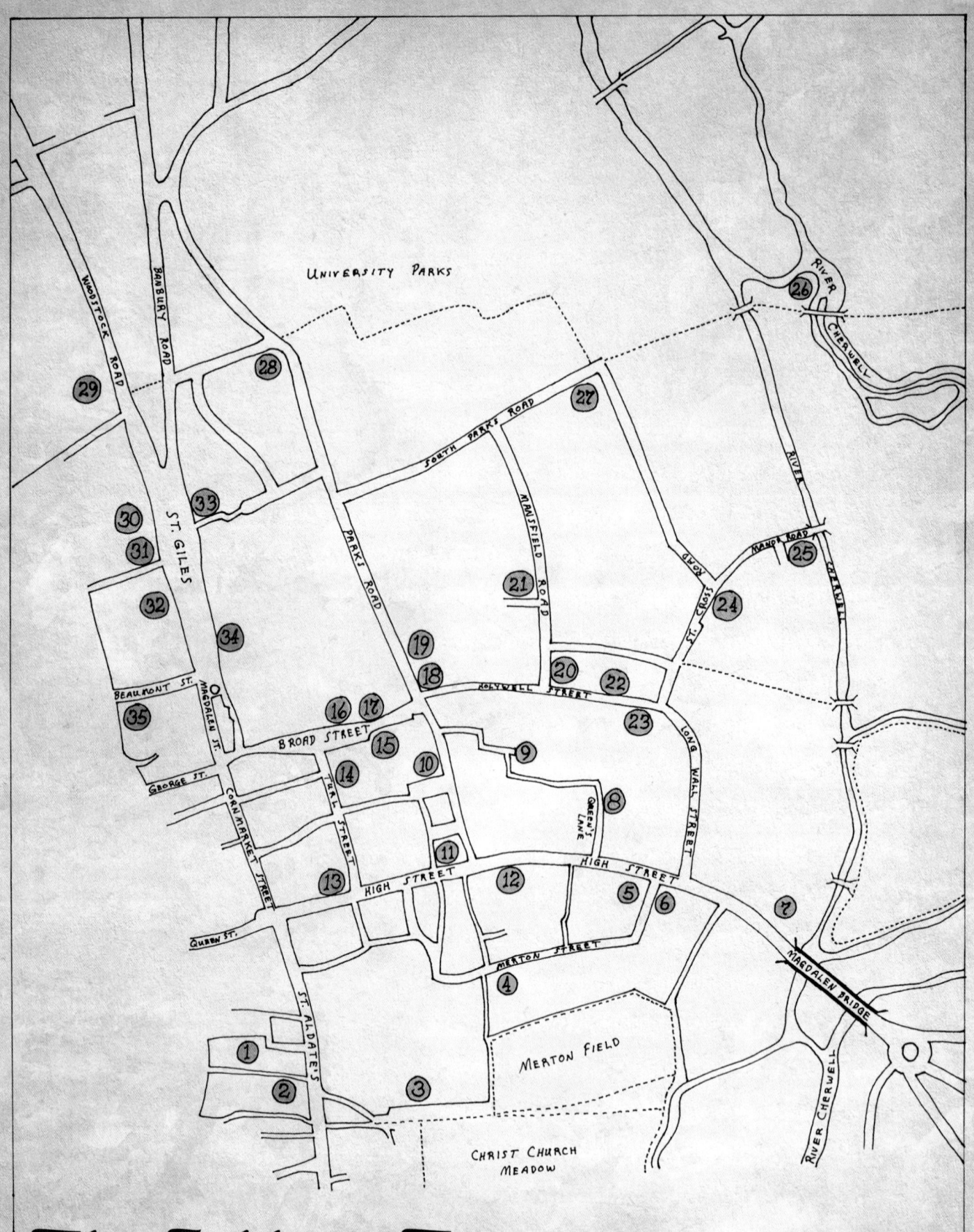

The Inklings Tour
of the City of Oxford

drawn by Harry Lee Poe

more block away from the Carfax. Cross the street and enter the great iron gates that lead to **Christ Church Meadow** ➤, where Alice followed a white rabbit down a hole to Wonderland. ③ To the left stands ◄ **Christ Church College** where Lord David Cecil spent his undergraduate days. The visitor's entrance is along this side wall. If you stop for a visit, turn left when you leave.

Follow the broad footpath along the side of the great stone walls of Christ Church. Turn left at the end of the wall and follow the footpath along the edge of the wall until you reach the iron gates. Go through the iron gates along the shaded footpath that leads to Merton Street. ④ Turn right onto Merton Street where you will find **Merton College** ➤ on the right. J. R. R. Tolkien moved to Merton College in 1945 with Hugo Dyson. Visitors enter by the main gate.

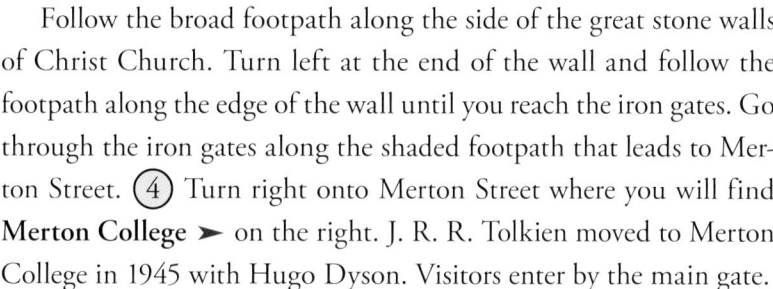

Upon leaving Merton College, turn right on Merton Street until it turns left and reaches the High Street. ⑤ On the left side of the street stands the ◄ **University Examination Schools Building**, where Lewis, Tolkien, and Cecil often lectured, and ⑥ on the right stands the **Eastgate Hotel** ➤ where Lewis and Tolkien met on Monday mornings for over twenty years until Lewis moved to Cambridge.

Turn right on High Street and continue down the street to the crosswalk. Cross the street and continue walking away from the Eastgate Hotel. ⑦ The imposing college and grounds on the left is ◄ **Magdalen College** where C. S. Lewis spent almost thirty years. Visitors enter by the main gate. Be sure to allow time to stroll along **Addison's Walk** ➤.

Upon leaving Magdalen, turn right at the gate and proceed along High Street. Enjoy the shops, but pay attention to the gradually unfolding vista of the towers along High Street as they curve into view. Turn right onto Queen's Lane. On the right stands little St. Edmund Hall. ⑧ Within the grounds of St. Edmund stands the ancient church building ◄ (**St. Peter's-in-the-East**), where Jack and Warnie Lewis went for Communion on Wednesday mornings. The building now serves as the library for St. Edmund. Visitors enter through the porter's lodge of St. Edmund.

Upon leaving St. Edmund, turn right and proceed along the narrow lane edged by high stone walls. Follow the lane as it turns left and then right. ⑨ At the next intersection, turn right to the old gate of New College where Lord David Cecil and Christopher Tolkien were fellows. Visitors enter through this gate.

Walking Tour 2: From New College to Wadham College

Upon leaving New College, proceed along the lane away from St. Edmund. This lane goes under the ◄ **Bridge of Sighs** and ends opposite the iron-fence-enclosed yard of the Clarendon Building. Turn left onto Catte Street. ⑩ The tall building on the right with the massive oak gates is the **Bodleian Library** ➤. Visitors may take a guided tour and see the ◄ **Divinity School**, which Lewis considered the most beautiful room in Oxford. Upon leaving the Bodleian through the main gate, turn right and walk past the round **Radcliffe Camera** ➤, a reading room of the Bodleian, to ⑪ ◄ **St. Mary the Virgin**, the University Church. From this pulpit Lewis preached "Learning in War-Time" and "The Weight of Glory." The Tower of St. Mary's offers a grand view of Oxford. Exit the church on the opposite side from which you entered, and step onto High Street.

Turn left upon leaving the church and cross the street. ⑫ The college standing in the curve of the street is **University College** ➤ where C. S. Lewis spent his undergraduate days. The college does not normally allow visitors, but the porter may allow you to look inside the front quad.

Upon leaving University College, return to St. Mary's and proceed toward the Carfax for one block. ⑬ On the corner of High Street and Turl Street stands the ◄ **Mitre**, a favorite eating spot for the Inklings, which still serves meals.

Turn onto Turl Street and proceed to the second block on the right. ⑭ The college on the right is **Exeter College** ➤ where J. R. R. Tolkien, Neville Coghill, and Hugo Dyson were undergraduates. Visitors enter at the porter's lodge. Notice the ◄ **bust of Tolkien** in the chapel.

Upon leaving Exeter, turn right and proceed to Broad Street. Turn right on Broad until an iron fence curves out into the walk. ⑮ Enter the gate to the Sheldonian Theatre, designed by Sir Christopher Wren, where all the great ceremonies of the university take place. Here Lewis delivered his winning English essay as an undergraduate and Tolkien received his honorary doctorate. Visitors enter the door in the center of the building closest to Broad Street. Climb the wooden stairs to the cupola for a splendid view of the Radcliffe Camera and St. Mary's tower.

⑯ Across Broad Street behind its iron fence stands **Trinity College** ➤ where Austin Farrer served as chaplain and the Tolkien boys were undergraduates. ⑰ On the same side of the street as Trinity stands the small White Horse Pub sandwiched between extensions of the sprawling Blackwell's Bookshop. This was one of the pubs

where the Inklings found refuge during the war. ⑱ At the end of Broad Street, on the other side of Blackwell's, stands the King's Arms, another pub where the Inklings could find beer when the Eagle and Child ran out. ⑲ Next to the King's Arms on Parks Road stands **Wadham College** ➤, where Lord David Cecil held a fellowship in the 1920s.

Walking Tour 3: From the King's Arms to the Oxford Playhouse

Return to the King's Arms and turn left onto Holywell Street. Note the ◄ **Holywell Music Room** on the left where the Inklings often attended concerts. At the end of the first block, turn left onto Mansfield Road. ⑳ On the right stands the **narrow, crooked house** ➤ where young Jack Lewis spent his first night in Oxford. Continue past this house across the street to the corner of Saville and Mansfield Road. ㉑ The large building on the left on Mansfield Road is Saville House, where Lord David Cecil had a flat.

Return to Holywell Street and turn left. ㉒ Hugo Dyson lived in the house at 12 Holywell. ㉓ Continue past Dyson's house to the end of the street, across the street, at ◄ **99 Holywell**, where Tolkien lived. After leaving Tolkien's house, turn left onto St. Cross Road. Go to the second block and cross the street at the crosswalk and continue walking away from Holywell.

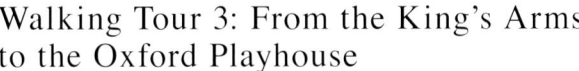

㉔ On the right stands **St. Cross Church** ➤ with its wild churchyard. Charles Williams, Hugo Dyson, and Austin Farrer lie buried here. A posted map of the churchyard provides directions to their graves through the tangle of brambles and nettles now maintained as a wildlife refuge.

Upon leaving the churchyard, turn right and proceed onto Manor Road. In the next block stands a row of houses. ㉕ The Tolkiens moved to **3 Manor Road** ➤ at the end of World War II. Cross the street and walk back to St. Cross Road. Turn right and walk the long stretch to South Parks Road. Turn right onto the footpath just past Linacre College. Continue along the footpath until you cross a small waterway. ㉖ Here the River Cherwell forks at ◄ **Parson's Pleasure** where Lewis and generations of undergraduates used to swim. Return to the road.

Proceeding straight from the footpath, you enter South Parks Road. ㉗ On the left corner where the Zoology and Psychology building now stands, Charles Williams boarded with the Spalding family. Continue along South Parks Road past Rhodes House to Parks Road and turn right. ㉘ Across the street in the next block

stands ◄ **Keble College** where Jack Lewis and Paddy Moore received their officer training and where Austin Farrer later served as warden. Past Keble College, turn left onto Keble Road and continue to Banbury Road. Cross Banbury Road at the crosswalk and follow the footpath through St. Giles churchyard to Woodstock Road. Cross Woodstock Road and turn right.

㉙ Just past the shops on the left stands the entry at the porter's lodge to **Somerville College** ➤, where Dorothy L. Sayers spent her undergraduate days and Stella Aldwinckle served in the chaplaincy. Next to Sommerville College on Woodstock Road is ◄ **St. Aloysius Church**, where the Tolkiens and Havards attended. After leaving Sommerville College, turn right on Woodstock Road and proceed to the next block, where Woodstock becomes St. Giles. ㉚ Halfway down the block, on the right side, stands the **Eagle and Child** ➤, where the Inklings met on Tuesday mornings until Lewis went to Cambridge, when they changed their day to Monday. Turn right when you leave the Eagle and Child and walk to the corner. ㉛ In this block of buildings now owned by Regent's Park College, the Tolkiens had a flat when Tolkien worked on the Oxford Dictionary.

Continue along St. Giles away from the Eagle and Child to the next block. ㉜ On the right stands ◄ **Blackfriars**, where Gervase Mathew was a member of the order. Cross St. Giles with great care and turn left. ㉝ On the right side of the street opposite the Eagle and Child stands the **Lamb and Flag** ➤, where the Inklings moved in the 1960s during renovations to the Eagle and Child. After leaving the Lamb and Flag, retrace your steps back down St. Giles, past where you crossed the street. ㉞ On the left side stands **St. John's College** ➤, where John Wain held a research fellowship. Be sure to visit the gardens of St. John's.

After leaving St. John's, turn left and continue away from the Lamb and Flag. Cross St. Giles again at the crosswalk that leads to the Randolph Hotel at the corner of St. Giles and Beaumont Street. ㉟ Walk in front of the Randolph, away from St. Giles, until you come to the ◄ **Oxford Playhouse** on the corner. Neville Coghill staged *Dr. Faustus* here in collaboration with his protégé, Richard Burton, who starred in the production with his wife, Elizabeth Taylor.

If you are still on your feet at this point, you shouldn't be. Go find a nice cup of tea, or perhaps something else, at one of the Inklings' many watering holes.

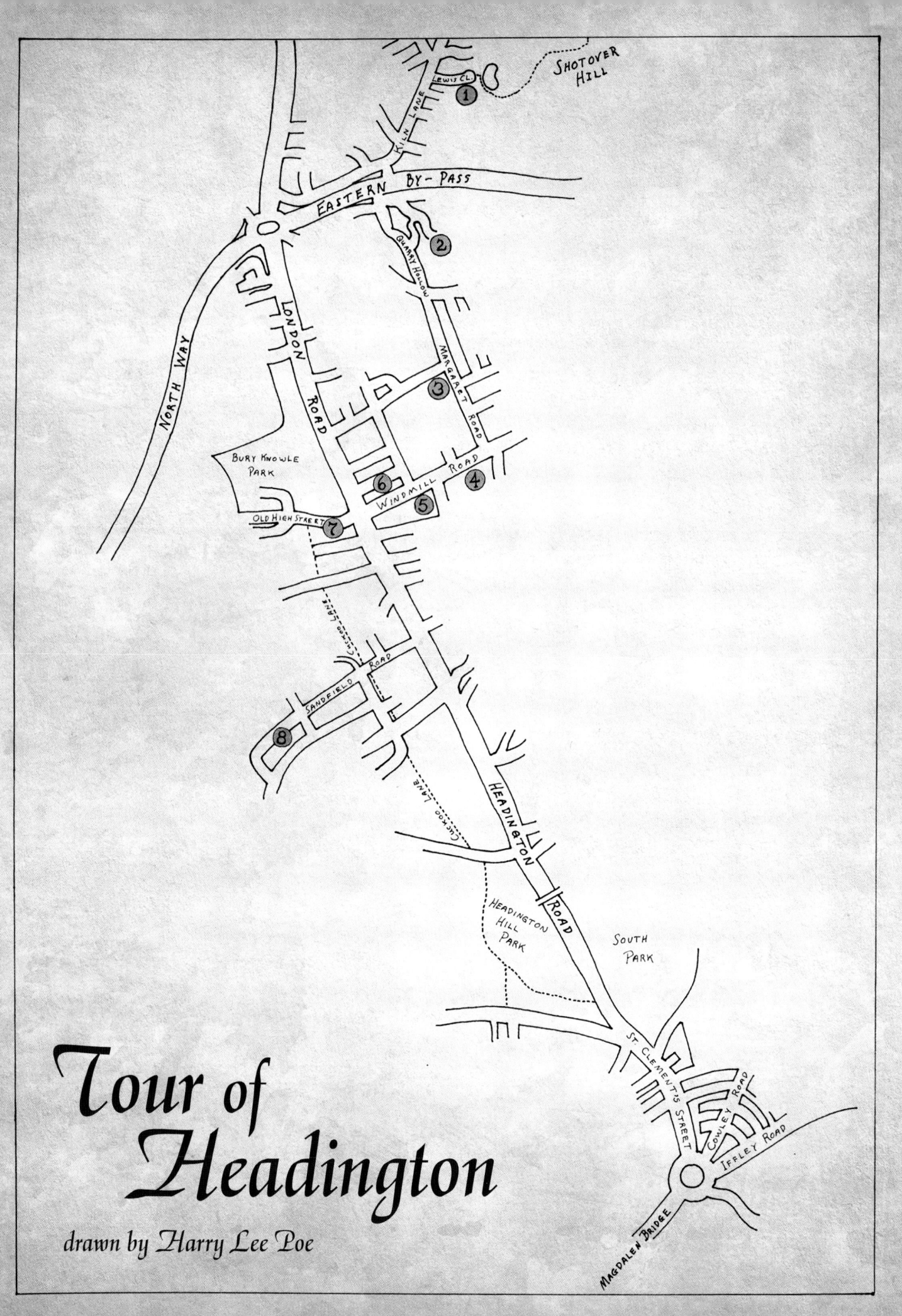

Tour of Headington

drawn by Harry Lee Poe

TOUR OF HEADINGTON (INCLUDING THE KILNS)

Walking Tour 4: Headington and the Kilns

The village of Headington to the east of Oxford, on the London Road, was home to C. S. Lewis and his brother, Major Warren Lewis, from 1931 until their deaths. It was also the home of J. R. R. Tolkien and his wife, Edith, from 1953 until 1968. The easiest way to reach Headington is by bus from Queen's Street beside the Carfax Tower. A row of bus stops lines the street with a sign at each stop that indicates the destination of the bus. Look for the bus to Headington/Risinghurst. Ask the driver for a ticket to the Lewis Close stop on Kilns Lane. (The full walking tour will involve a stroll all the way back to Oxford. If you do not feel up to this much fun, ask the driver for a "return ticket.")

(1) When you step from the bus, walk in the direction the bus travels and turn right onto Lewis Close. ◄ **The Kilns** is the first house on the right side of the street. During the lifetime of C. S. Lewis, the entire street was part of the Kilns property, but when he died, his brother sold off lots for development, so fearful was he that he would not have enough money for his old age. You may stand on the street and see Lewis's home, but if you would like a tour of the interior, you should call ahead for an appointment since the home is used by the C. S. Lewis Foundation as a study center for visiting scholars (for information: www.cslewis.org).

After visiting the house, turn right upon leaving the gate and enter the nature preserve that begins at the edge of the Close with a path to the pond where Lewis used to swim. He cut the paths through this wild area and planted many of the trees. At the left end of the pond is the ◄ **bomb shelter** Lewis had built at the beginning of World War II. At the right end of the pond stands the semicircular brick bench Lewis built for enjoying the view of the pond. Climb the path to the right of the bench to the top of **Shotover Hill** ➤ and a view of the surrounding countryside.

When you finish your walk on the hill, return down Lewis Close to Kilns Lane and turn left. Proceed down Kilns Lane all the way to the Eastern By-Pass. Do not follow the curve of the road to the right. (2) Cross the Eastern By-Pass at the crossing lights where you will reach Trinity Road, which winds its way a short distance to **Holy Trinity Church** ➤, where Jack and Warnie Lewis attended services every Sunday. Both brothers lie buried together under a single gravestone. Walk straight into the churchyard past the church to the back wall, where a sign points to the left directing you to the Lewis grave. After visiting the grave, enter the church. Along the far outside aisle

you will find the ◄ **short pew** where the Lewis brothers habitually sat. It is on the left side of the church facing the altar, about half-way back, next to a stone column opposite the board that posts the psalms. It is marked by a small brass plaque. When you have finished your visit, return to Trinity Road and turn left.

After only a few feet, turn left onto Quarry School Road. At the end of this short street, turn left onto Quarry Hollow and climb the hill where the name changes to Margaret Road. ③ Continue along Margaret Road to the intersection of Wharton Road where the **Catholic Church of Corpus Christi** ➤ stands on the corner. The Tolkiens attended this church when they lived in Headington. Continue along Margaret Road to Windmill Road and turn right. ④ Across the road at ◄ **76 Windmill Road**, Janie Moore and her daughter, Maureen, lived for a short time. ⑤ Continue until you reach **58 Windmill Road** ➤ on the left. Lewis lived here with the Moores for a short time. Continue up the road to the London Road.

Turn right on the London Road and walk to Holyoake Street. ⑥ Turn right and walk the short distance to **number 14** ➤. A carved stone on the side of the two-story brick house reads "Hillsboro House." Lewis and the Moores lived here from August 1, 1922, until they moved to the Kilns almost ten years later. Return to the London Road and turn left. Walk back to Windmill Road and turn right to cross the London Road. On this side of the London Road the name of the street changes to Old High Street. ⑦ Walk to ◄ **number 10 Old High Street** on the left side of the street. The two-story semi-detached house is where Joy Gresham and her sons lived before they moved to the Kilns. Joy's home is the right side of the building.

Proceed away from the London Road on Old High Street, just past Joy's house, where you will see a small footpath on the left. This is **Cuckoo Lane** ➤. This path runs from Headington to the river opposite Magdalen College. Turn left onto Cuckoo Lane and continue for several long blocks to Sandfield Road. ⑧ Turn right and go to ◄ **76 Sandfield Road** on the left side of the street. The two-story white stucco house is where Ronald and Edith Tolkien lived for fifteen years. Note the stone marker on the side of the house.

For those who have walked enough, turn around and walk to the end of Sandfield. Cross the street to the bus stop where any bus will take you back to the city center. For the more stout of spirit, turn right onto Cuckoo Lane and walk all the way back to Oxford. You will cross several streets, pass woodlands and garden plots, and finally reach a fork in the path. Go straight for Headington Parks or turn right for a more roundabout return.

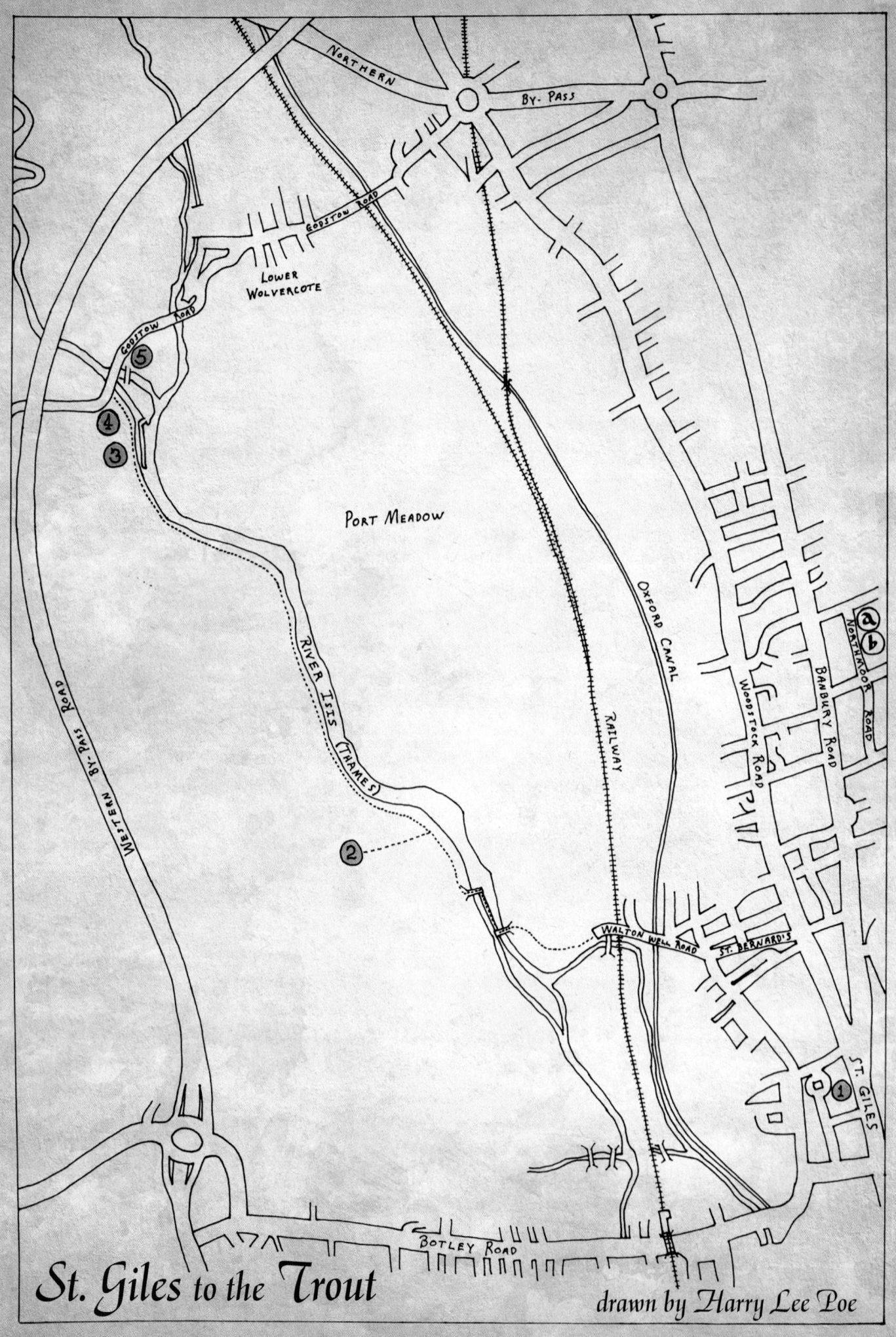

St. Giles to the Trout

drawn by Harry Lee Poe

A Tour from St. Giles to the Trout

The Trout at Godstow

◄ **The Trout** on the river at Lower Wolvercote was a favorite dining spot for the Inklings. It is an ambitious walk for those who have grown lazy, but it is a rewarding venture with its footpath along the river, across open meadows from Oxford to the medieval abbey at Godstow. (1) From the Eagle and Child pub in St. Giles take the Woodstock Road to the left, where St. Giles forks at the War Memorial.

As you continue along the Woodstock Road, notice the old Radcliffe Infirmary and the stately Radcliffe Observatory on the left, followed by Green College. Across the street from Green College on the right is St. Anne's College, one of the houses established in the late nineteenth century to educate women.

Just beyond Green College, turn left onto St. Bernard's Road. Continue to the intersection with Kingston Road and proceed across the road onto Walton Well Road, which intersects at an angle from the northwest. Proceed along Walton Well Road over the Oxford Canal and the railroad line into **Port Meadow** ➤, which stretches far away to the north. Here the road ends and the footpath begins.

Follow the footpath to the river and cross among the docked boats at Rainbow Bridge. Turn to the right upon crossing the bridge and proceed along the footpath that borders the river. Along the way you will see ducks, geese, and swans plying their way along the river.

A pathway enters the footpath from the left soon after leaving Rainbow Bridge. (2) This path may have a sign that indicates the riverside entrance to the Perch, a hospitable pub where the Inklings often broke their trip to the Trout with some refreshment. The Perch offers a variety of beverages as well as food that may be enjoyed within its medieval walls under its neatly thatched roof or outside in its well maintained garden.

Continuing the journey northward along the river, you will encounter several gates intended to keep the cattle in the meadow. Mind the evidence of cows as you walk along. (3) Eventually you will come to the old lock at Godstow. Take a moment to examine how the system of locks and canals created an inland waterway before the advent of the steam locomotive. The week before Hitler invaded Poland, several of the Inklings used Warnie Lewis's boat, the Bosphorus, to explore this river from ◄ **Folly Bridge** for thirty miles up river. They traveled along this route and stopped at the Trout for supper.

④ Just beyond the Godstow Lock, on the left, stands the ruins of the ◄ **medieval Godstow Abbey** where Henry II kept his beautiful mistress, fair Rosalind, who died mysteriously here at Godstow. Henry's wife, Eleanor of Aquitaine, denied that she had poisoned fair Rosalind. It was at the court of Eleanor, in her possessions in France, where courtly love poetry was born and blossomed. C. S. Lewis's first important book of scholarship, *The Allegory of Love*, was devoted to a study of this tradition.

Just beyond the abbey you will come to a paved but narrow road. Turn right and walk to the bridge. ⑤ Pause for a moment to admire the view of the river below and the Trout lying alongside it on the opposite shore. In this pool beside the Trout, divers recovered the Wolvercote Buckle in the Inspector Morse detective story.

Inside the Trout you will place your order at the counter where you will receive a number on a wooden paddle. You may enjoy your meal inside one of the old rooms warmed by a fire in many months of the year, or outside by the river in good weather.

For the less ambitious traveler, the Trout may be reached by taxi from Oxford, which is less than four miles from St. Giles. Bus service also goes to Wolvercote, but a short walk to the west of town will be necessary to reach the Trout.

28

In our busy world, most of us travel by automobile on our daily rounds. The Inklings walked. You have now walked the streets and paths that they walked every day. Many changes have come to Oxford since I first saw it the year that Warnie Lewis and J. R. R. Tolkien died, but you have seen much that the Inklings would have known and loved. You have seen it as they saw it – on foot.

NOTES

1. Owen Barfield, "C. S. Lewis as Christian and Scholar," *C. S. Lewis Remembered: Collected Reflections of Students, Friends, and Colleagues*, ed. Harry Lee Poe and Rebecca Whitten Poe (Grand Rapids: Zondervan, 2006), 35.

2. Lewis recounts this episode in his spiritual autobiography: C. S. Lewis, *Surprised by Joy* (New York: Harcourt, Brace, 1955), 17.

3. Ibid., 170.

4. Ibid., 191.

5. Ibid., 197 – 98.

6. Ibid., 198.

7. C. S. Lewis, *The Collected Letters of C. S. Lewis*, ed. Walter Hooper (New York: HarperSanFrancisco, 2004), I:970.

8. Ibid., I:977.

9. Ibid.

10. Lewis, *Surprised by Joy*, 237

11. Lewis mentions the Martlets in a letter to his father on February 4, 1919. See Lewis, *Letters*, I:430. In a letter of March 5, 1919, he indicated that he was writing a paper on William Morris for the Martlets (I:443). Walter Hooper discusses the history of the Martlets in *Through Joy and Beyond* (New York: Macmillan, 1982), 67.

12. Lewis, *Letters*, I:778.

13. Ibid., I:732.

14. Ibid.

15. Ibid., II:287 – 288.

16. Humphrey Carpenter, *The Inklings* (New York: Ballentine, 1981), 61.

17. Humphrey Carpenter, *Tolkien* (Boston: Houghton Mifflin, 1977), 45 – 46.

18. Ibid., 102.

19. Lewis, *Letters*, II:9.

20. Ibid., II:306.

21. Ibid., II:365.

22. J. R. R. Tolkien, *The Letters of J. R. R. Tolkien*, ed. Humphrey Carpenter and Christopher Tolkien (Boston: Houghton Mifflin, 1981), 387 – 88.

23. Carpenter, *The Inklings*, 179.

24. George Sayers, *Jack: C. S. Lewis and His Times* (New York: Harper & Row, 1988), 112.

25. Lewis, *Letters*, II:293.

26. Ibid.

27. Ibid., II:355.

28. Ibid., II:183.

29. Ibid., II:219 – 220.

30. Tolkien, *The Letters of J. R. R. Tolkien*, 29.

31. Ibid., 36.

32. Lewis, *Letters*, II:288 – 289.

33. Ibid., II:16.

34. Lewis made this observation in a letter to Ruth Pitter in 1947. See Lewis, *Letters*, II:753.

35. C. S. Lewis, *Out of the Silent Planet* (New York: Macmillan, 1965), 27.

36. Lewis, *Letters*, II:594.

37. Lewis, *Out of the Silent Planet*, 35.

38. C. S. Lewis, *The Allegory of Love* (New York: Galaxy, 1958), 68, 69.

39. Carpenter, *Tolkien*, 81.

40. Lewis, *Letters*, II:160n.

41. Warnie Lewis discusses the annual January walking tours in his diaries. See Clyde S. Kilby and Marjorie Lamp Mead, eds., *Brothers and Friends: The Diaries of Major Warren Hamilton Lewis* (New York: Harper & Row, 1982), 76, 96, 132, 136, 167, 171, 174 – 175.

42. Ibid., 35 – 37, 62.

43. Ibid., 35, 37, 57, 62.

44. C. S. Lewis, *Boxen*, ed. Walter Hooper (New York: Harcourt Brace Jovanovich, 1985), 61ff.

45. Kilby and Mead, *Brothers and Friends*, 174.

46. Dr. Robert E. "Humphrey" Havard recorded his recollections of this trip, which are deposited in the Wade Collection at Wheaton College. James Como included Havard's recollections of Lewis as "Philia: Jack at Ease" in his important 1979 collection *C. S. Lewis at the Breakfast Table* and now published in its third edition as *Remembering C. S. Lewis: Recollections of Those Who Knew Him* (San Francisco: Ignatius, 2005), 349 – 67. Humphrey Carpenter cites Havard's recollection in his excellent book, *The Inklings*, 74 – 75.

47. C. S. Lewis, "Learning in War-Time," *The Weight of Glory*, ed. Walter Hooper (New York: Simon & Schuster, 1996), 42.

48. Ibid., 44.

49. Carpenter, *The Inklings*, 194.

50. Lewis, *Letters*, II:486.

51. Kilby and Mead, *Brothers and Friends*, 161.

52. Lewis describes the inspiration in a letter to Warnie dated July 20, 1940. See *Letters*, II:426.

53. Kilby and Mead, *Brothers and Friends*, 211.

54. Ibid., 147.

55. Carpenter, *The Letters of J. R. R. Tolkien*, 71.

56. Kilby and Mead, *Brothers and Friends*, 235.

57. Ibid., 181.

58. Lewis, *Letters*, II:399.

59. Ibid., II:432.

60. See Don W. King, "The Anatomy of a Friendship: The Correspondence of Ruth Pitter and C. S. Lewis, 1946 – 1962," *Mythlore*, 24:1 (Summer 2003), 3.

61. Ibid.

62. Lewis, *Letters*, II:365.

63. Kilby and Mead, *Brothers and Friends*, 182.

64. Lewis, *Letters*, II:16.

65. Kilby and Mead, *Brothers and Friends*, 193.

66. Ibid., 218.

67. Lewis, *Letters*, II:853.

68. Carpenter, *The Letters of J. R. R. Tolkien*, 102.

69. Humphrey Carpenter discusses the change of venue briefly in his two books, *The Inklings*, 203, and *Tolkien*, 197.

70. C. S. Lewis, *Miracles* (London: Geoffrey Bles, 1947), 27.

71. Derek Brewer, "The Tutor: A Portrait," *C. S. Lewis at the Breakfast Table*, ed. James T. Como (New York: Macmillan, 1985), 59.

72. Email from John Randolph Lucas to Jerry Walls, August 28, 2003.

73. Kilby and Mead, *Brothers and Friends*, 230.

74. Ibid., 236.

75. Carpenter, *Tolkien*, 219.

76. Ibid., 202.

77. J. R. R. Tolkien, *The Silmarillion* (New York: Ballantine Publishing Group, 1999).

78. Lecture by Emrys Jones, July 2002, C. S. Lewis Summer Institute, Oxford.

79. Theresa Whistler, "Working for David," *David Cecil: A Portrait by His Friends*, ed. Hannah Cranborne (Stanbridge, Dorset: Dovecote Press, 1991), 90 – 91.

80. Sayer, *Jack*, 211.

81. Ibid., 212.

82. Kilby and Mead, *Brothers and Friends*, 245.

83. Lewis, *Letters*, II:965.

We want to hear from you. Please send your comments about this
book to us in care of zreview@zondervan.com. Thank you.